&

# The Dance
# Between
# Hope & Fear

JOHN CALVI

The Dance Between Hope & Fear
True Quaker Press
Putney, Vermont
ISBN: 978-0-9893285-0-0

*I dedicate this book to you, dear husband Marshall, because your love has made all things possible. True love would have been enough, but you are also the fun, the delicious, the encyclopedic, and the balm in our life.*

"If there are no more questions, I'd like to make a statement. My book *Wisdom's Daughters* is about the women around Jesus. I had been immersed in the Gospels for more than twelve years in the course of writing the book, and I would come to the healing miracles—and I just didn't believe them. I thought, 'Well, this is exaggeration; this was another time.' And then I met John, and experienced myself the healing in his hands. Then I understood how Jesus healed.

"Now, I'm not equating John with a Christ figure, not after all he's told us about his life today, but he was a revelation to me about how Jesus healed. I vouch for the genuineness of his gift. I have experienced it."

~ Elizabeth Watson, 1914-2004. Quaker author of *Guests in My Life*, *Healing Ourselves and the Earth*, and *Wisdom's Daughters*, among many more. Speaking from the audience at the end of a teaching John gave at Guilford College in 1999.

# CONTENTS

Editor's Introduction      i

Editor Interviews Author      iii

Section 1. The Dance Between Hope & Fear      1

Section 2. Early Years      25

Section 3. The AIDS War Begins      53

Section 4. Hands On      81

Section 5. Healing Trauma      107

Section 6. From the Journals      143

Section 7. Home Life      165

Section 8. Healing America, Ending Torture      199

Permissions and Credits      218

Glossary of Quaker Terms      220

How Do You Say Thank You to Thousands?      224

# Editor's Introduction

John Calvi is well known among Quakers throughout North America. He may be equally well known in some other circles, but his is not generally a household name. And his vocation is not an ordinary one, even within Quaker circles. John is a Quaker healer.

*The Dance Between Hope & Fear* is by John and about John. It's not a how-to-do-healing book, but about how John came to spend, as this book arrives, a bit over thirty years as a Quaker healer and what he has learned—about himself, healing, spiritual honesty, and giving over to Divine leadings. This book is not just for Quakers. It's for anyone, as John Punshon says, "with a love of humanity in their heart."

The book begins with a Friends General Conference keynote speech given in 1990. The speech was a success in Quaker terms and was reprinted in *Each of Us Inevitable* as well as being a best selling recording in the FGC bookstore. This speech sets out John's early work up to that time.

The last section, "Healing America, Ending Torture," is John's 2011 FGC Plenary speech, *To Go Where There is No Light*, and contains information about the Quaker Initiative to End Torture (QUIT), which was founded by John and some good Friends.

Between the two speeches, in six sections, is a sampling of the voluminous articles, journal entries, observations, letters, songs, teachings, and whimsies written by John over thirty years.

*Section 2*, Early Years, relates some facets of John's movement into spiritual healing and what he was learning "on the job"— teaching, writing music, going to massage school, determining how to carry out his spiritual work, and working with tortured refugees. Dyslexic, barely able to scrape through high school, as John says of himself—what was leading him? It was in the early years that John decided those who needed healing work the most were least likely to be able to pay for it; his solution was to live mostly on invitations to teach and gifts from friends who wanted to be a part of his work.

*Section 3*, The AIDS War Begins, contains pieces from his journals and tells the story of John's work in the AIDS effort. During this time John's gift matured and his work increased. He saw hundreds of friends, his best friend, die. Through it all he sought and received greater spiritual clarity and began to realize what it means to take on large work for the long haul.

*Section 4*, Hands On, goes deeply into his inward experiences and lessons as a spiritual healer, as well as shedding light and Light on Quaker healers in general.

*Section 5*, Healing Trauma, differs from other sections of the book. These are not pieces from John's journals and are best read sequentially. Based on his own and the experience of others, John explains how trauma works within us, how we might heal, how we make space, and how healers—or any spiritual workers—might protect themselves from burnout. Those in the healing professions, those who hurt, those who grieve—all can find advice, solace, and encouragement.

*Section 6*, From the Journals, contains pieces included to show the diversity of communities that a Quaker healer, or anyone, might find in need of healing. Cambodian grandmothers, women of the Comadres, a small boy who witnessed the Oklahoma bombing—how does a healer address the differences and the similarities of their deep needs?

*Section 7*, Home Life, is the lightest of the sections. It may also be the most subtly profound for understanding John's ability to work in the worst of situations for so many years. Fifteen journal entries have been included to show the human balance that keeps a healer sane and able to work for decades. Food, love, warmth, community engagement, rest and retreat, aggravation, housework, nature, and humor round out the picture.

This book doesn't demand that you read it sequentially. If one part is too heavy, skip ahead to Section 7. If you feel ready for a deep plunge into the hurts of the world, read Sections 3 and 8. You will find you come back to some pieces over and over. Let Spirit lead you on the journey with John.

Shelly Angel
Editor

# Editor Interviews Author

*Shelly Angel: Can you tell us about becoming a Quaker? You were raised Catholic, and then something must have changed. What happened?*

John Calvi: It was the spring of 1968. I had just gotten my driver's license. A friend, Mel Ash, asked me to drive him to a Quaker Meeting a few towns over from where I lived on my grandmother's farm in Connecticut. Mel was creating an alternative high school newspaper and wanted to interview a man there who'd been a colonel in World War One.*

I had been attending Catholic mass and was the only person in my immediate family still going to church. But at sixteen, as a gay person, I could see that the church would not be a good spiritual home. And I knew spiritual life was always going to be important to me.

We went into a grand house at Wesleyan University. There were a dozen people gathered in silence with only a few spoken messages. I loved it immediately.

I'd seen one of the Quaker elders the night before at a program of Iroquois dances. Indians were teaching the rest of us the dances. But there was this one little elfin white guy who knew all the words to the songs. Turned out he was the clerk of the Quaker Meeting. That was David McAllester. David became my draft counselor when I registered as a conscientious objector (CO) at eighteen.

I began to go to Quaker Meeting every Sunday. I would go to the back row of folding chairs and lie on the carpet. It was as though I was soaking in a bath of peaceful silence, being washed of all the noise in my life and taking in the calm and quiet. I don't know what the Quakers thought. But it was a university Meeting, so I think they were accustomed to odd young people coming and going.

I began to sense the essences within Quakerism, though in those teen years I mostly just took in the calm and quiet—which the older Friends had in good supply—to survive a difficult adolescence.

* Mel Ash is the author of The Zen of Recovery, Shaving the Inside of Your Skull, and Beat Spirit.

I became a CO and listened to the messages given in Meeting very carefully. I believe this engendered in me the desire for a life of the mind, with a spiritual posture of seeking and with constant wonder as a way to be in the world. This was a great comfort to me, being completely contrary to home life, high school, and the church.

A dozen years later I would discover an organization of gay Quakers where I made lifelong friends and joined a community of seekers who also understood that the oppression of gay people was morally wrong.

All this was a boost to understanding the world very differently from how it formerly seemed; I was able to feel and know myself and my world more honestly than simply repeating what I'd been told. For me this was the essence of the 1950's transformed by the cultural shift of the 1960's.

*SA: Were there other circumstances that set you apart on a journey, a journey larger than your awareness at the time?*

JC: My mother's mother had eleven children, and I have twenty-one first cousins on that side of the family. Among my large extended family, church was something one went to on Sunday. As working class people there was no delving into charitable work or learning about other people's struggles to live. One lived honestly and simply, and tried to be a good person. Family was the primary source of community and values. It was very much an Italian enclave on a large farm of five households at the end of the road in a small town. The extended family was a large happy crowd and the farm was a great place to grow up. It was also constraining and resistant to change and newness.

It was rare for someone in the family to step outside or to leave the tribe to live elsewhere. Most of the family is still within easy driving distance of the farm. But I had to leave home to unfold toward my best self. I realized that I needed space to discover the various aspects I was noticing in me and live on my own without the gravity of tradition to grind me down. Being gay was illegal and still strictly considered a serious mental illness; being a Quaker and against war in a family of veterans, being a learning-disabled young person who was unfit for college but sought life beyond working class jobs—all this had to be worked out away from the family, experimented within the outside world.

I left home at eighteen and never lived there again. The capacity to sit in silence and be open to wonder and guidance without hearing only myself made all of this transition in my life possible. What is necessary now? And what do I want life to be like next? This spacious silence was the gift of Quakers in my life. This posture of seeking and being open to the heart's desire and to change was not just hopeful youth. It was also choosing new paths over selfish paths of indulgence or the desire to make the most money possible. I wanted to release all of my creative self and to work for less pain and confusion in myself, people I knew, and my country.

*SA: What was the effect of becoming and being a Quaker on your gift as a healer?*

JC: I became a performing musician first and then a Montessori teacher as a young adult. Teaching young children showed me that I had a gift to share calm. And I felt great joy in helping a child come to a place of less fear and more trust. It was a kind of high I can't describe. To have good relationships with two dozen children in my care was probably the hardest and most rewarding work I've ever done.

I have a similar experience in Quaker Meeting for worship. Sitting in the stillness, quieting my mind to stop hearing my own voice, and listening to the quiet feels like coming to a point of trust within myself—a trust that I can feel all of myself and still sit peaceably. Yes, there might be some large emotions. And I may have to feel several of them crowding all together. But after a time I can also feel these emotions turn to peace, undiminished in importance yet not so demanding. This discipline gives me enough quiet of mind to hear guidance, the messages that come regarding healing work.

A special preparation in the classroom for my later work was that I could be with the pain and confusion of others and keep my calm. Children depended on this and parents did too. As I began to feel a leading for healing work, this discipline of calm from both teaching and Quakerism gave me a foundation to work from.

*SA: When did you first realize that your healing work was different from being just a soothing massage?*

JC: I think there were many small beginnings, signs along the way. Helping my cousins sooth the pain of nettles at age five, being a young person that adults confided in, early in my life being able to feel in others a larger sense of their emotional life than they might be conscious of—I see these as pointing to a possible future in healing work.

But there was a particular time I think of as the point when my healing work really began. I'd had some tutoring in massage and was soon to enter massage school, but hadn't had formal training as yet. I was thirty, and a good friend complained of a nervous stomach. She wasn't sleeping at night, was often nauseated, and couldn't keep food down. Doctors had found no physical cause for these symptoms.

As she lay on the massage table, I slowly worked over her muscles. She was a strong athletic young woman. When I came to her belly, I felt a rush of emotion move through me. My hands became very warm, and she began to shake a bit and later to weep. Much of the pain was actually fear and tension contracting the body, and this was relieved not only by working the muscles with massage, but with drawing that extra energy away so the muscle could relax deeply in an immediate way. At the end of the massage she told me she had suddenly regained a memory of abduction and torture as a teenager. There were burns on her body revealing some of the abuse. She began to feel better soon afterward—but then, of course, had to work with this new knowledge. She and I are still close friends.

It would take me several months to understand what happened that evening. A gift of release had been given her through my touch work. This was the most obvious beginning I can recall. Soon several rape survivors came for work from me during my time at massage school.

It took me over a year, experiencing this over and over, before I understood in some articulate fashion that pain was being released from the bodywork at an energetic level. I did understand it as a spiritual gift. And the more I surrendered to it and studied it in that framework, the more work came to me and the more I learned over time.

Now it's thirty years later and not only have I made this gift my life's work, I've lived mainly on gifts and worked by invitation as a teacher and healer. No one is more surprised than I am.

# Section 1

# The Dance Between
# Hope & Fear

## CLOSING KEYNOTE ADDRESS

## FRIENDS GENERAL CONFERENCE

Carlton College, Carlton, Minnesota

## 1990

# The Dance Between Hope & Fear

*Dear Great and Holy Spirit, be with me now as I do this work. May I be guided by your wisdom that I may receive comfort, healing, and protection. May I be a vessel of your love. Thank you for this opportunity to love.*

This is how I go to work in the morning. And it is a great honor and excitement for me to be with you tonight. It's also a bit too much—a bit too overwhelming—and I wouldn't want to do it without some help from friends in high places.

I'm genuinely amazed at how much I don't know. There are all kinds of things that I truly do not know about. I was about twenty-six before it finally occurred to me that the second hand on the clock was called that because it showed the seconds. I kept wondering why it wasn't called the third hand.

But I do know about healing. I know about it as a result of working in the AIDS epidemic for seven years, and working with refugees who have been tortured. I am going to speak to you tonight from my experience and only from my experience. I want to talk with you about some prerequisites for healing for an individual, for a Meeting, for a situation. I speak to you not only as a certified massage therapist and a Quaker healer, but as someone who has survived rape as a young child, and a family that was ruined by alcoholism and violence. I speak to you as a gay man, married under the care of my Meeting, living in a world that destroys gay people every day.

## Surrendering

One of the first things needed for healing is surrender, surrendering to deep feeling—feeling the depth of sadness and of loss, the depth of terror, of anger—feeling very, very deeply, more deeply than is comfortable, more deeply than people would like to, ever. That great surrender that all of us have felt at some time in Meeting when we finally saw that thing that we really didn't want to look at. The surrender when an entire Meeting sees what has been blocking the way and what made it impossible to see for a long time. So often I feel like I'm sitting in a chair in the corner with my hands over my eyes, complaining to God that I can't see anything.

Among us are some very sensitive people. Very often we call these people hypersensitive, and when they are not in our presence, we call them hysterical. I tend to be an independent sort of person who does things on his own. I really am not very good at huddling in a group trying to make group decisions. And when someone gets very sensitive in their thoughts and feelings, and becomes physically demonstrative in the way they're expressing themselves, part of me wants to say, "Shut up and roll up your sleeves." But with hindsight, I can see very clearly that it is the extremely sensitive people who let us know what's going on deep within ourselves. I need to keep reminding myself: *Blessed are the tenderhearted for they reveal to us our deepest feelings.*

When people are having hard times, one of the first things that happens is they start to close down in their bodies—in the ways they move and in the ways they talk to one another. People actually get smaller in their bodies, because times are hard. The idea of surrendering, of feeling deeply, sounds like leaning into a punch. But it is these very tenderhearted people who are the first to do it. That act of surrender is the first piece of work—feeling how deeply we are hurt, how much trouble we are in, feeling deeply how much danger is around us. That's always the first work, because we can't go anywhere without that initial assessment. Are we into it up to our armpits? Yes. OK, now that we have that clarity we can begin some work.

Let me sing you a song I wrote some years ago when I first was beginning to work in the AIDS epidemic. I was looking to put together my rule of things I needed to remember so I could recall, while in the midst of very painful situations, how to make a gift without taking on the sadness and despair of that situation.

### A Little Gracefulness

Sometimes I remember,
sometimes I forget,
you want to do something wonderful,
takes a little gracefulness.
It takes a little quiet,
it takes a little joy, joy, joy,
takes some believing in good.

Takes a little gracefulness
to let the love in, in, in.
Takes a little gracefulness
to let it go again.
it takes a little sadness,
and feeling your stuff, stuff, stuff,
to feel when way opens.
Takes a little gracefulness.

I believe there's plenty.
I believe that you care.
I believe in me
and the sun that's always shining somewhere.
Takes a little quiet.
Takes a little joy, joy, joy.
Takes some believing in good.
Sometimes I remember.

## Inviting Angels

In my experience, the next part of healing is inviting angels. I have a sense that each of us has some friends in high places, and I don't go to work without them, I really don't. All of us have friends all around us all the time. It's very important during hard times to sit still and say, "If you would be so kind, I need some more understanding. I need some patience. Maybe I need a little bit more time."

Very often trouble comes in a form a little bit like playing tennis: You know, they hit the ball at you, and it's coming down over there. And what do you know about getting the racquet over there in order to get the ball back to the other side?

Trouble can also seem like some sort of life quiz. "OK, I'm sending you this trouble. What do you know? What do you know about life?" And when we don't know enough, we can say, "Excuse me, about this quiz you sent. I know that this is the second time I've flunked it. Could we, like, do the lesson again a little bit? One more time? Slower?"

Sometimes I imagine my angels are like my great uncles and aunts, sitting around a card table up on a cloud. And one of them says, "I know! Let's get him ready to do this thing over here." But another one says, "Oh, no! He's not ready for that! Look at him. Look what happens to him when he doesn't find parking in front of the laundromat. He's not ready for that big thing over there."

If you're going to invite your angels, you need a certain level of softness. When I began doing my work, I really didn't have very much belief in angels. Then one day I was working with a healer, a wonderful woman by the name of Jean Schweitzer, who could look into your body as easily as if she were looking into a glass milk bottle. And she told me, "Well, now, you have some very big angels with you, and you can always ask for help."

One day I was not ready to do the work that came to me: three people, one right after another, who were in big trouble. But it was very much like the parable of the loaves and fishes. The energy I needed to do what was being asked of me came to me, so that I could make a beautiful gift to them. Afterward I sat down in meditation and prayer and said, "Now see here, what is going on? I don't really believe in angels, but I could sort of feel you there, so I wish you would show up and talk to me, because I'm going down this road in a way that I don't understand."

The angels wouldn't show up until I cried—until I felt the depth and the deep quiet that one needs to hear angels. Some angels came right through, and they said, "Now see here, we're going to get a lot of work done." "Well, what am I supposed to do?" "All you have to do is stay soft. In your tenderness, you can receive these gifts, and you can give them to others, and you must invite us."

Let me sing you a song called "Carry and Burn." I wrote it a while ago when I was up in Vermont, hauling firewood. This song came to me as I was realizing that someone who is making a gift through healing is doing the very same type of work as the person being worked on. Everyone who is looking to be of help and everyone helped is involved in the same task, being as graceful and as wise as they can be in a situation that is invariably organized against grace and wisdom.

### Carry and Burn

Carry and burn.
Carry and burn.
This firewood I gather
to carry and burn.
And my love is the same,
oh, my love is the same.
We gather and gather
to carry and burn.

I'm afraid of the fire
It will change me, I know.
What will be left
when I pass through
of the me I know now?
What will be new?

Like any love it undresses you
and gives too much,
and asks much more than you have.
And the view from here
and the view from here
is more, more than one chooses.

## Receiving Messages

I have always been very reluctant to receive messages, because I know that it's going to mean more work. When I first began to receive what I understood to be clear messages, I had a great deal of reluctance to hear them. I thought, "Well now, I'm just a nice working-class Italian-American kid, and I really would prefer not to do anything too New Age-y or too old-fashioned." But, you know, if the voices get loud, they get *loud*!

When people are having hard times, when a Meeting is having a hard time, they want to get up and do something. They want to blame other people. So it becomes even more important to sit down and be quiet; to listen very carefully, and try not to hear yourself.

Messages are very sneaky things. They come in ways that you don't expect. I imagine just about everybody here has bumped into some large thing that was a very clear message to slow down.

Once upon a time, I was in a thrift store. I saw an entire rack of ancient suitcases, and all of a sudden, I knew that I was supposed to buy some of them. So here I am, standing in the Salvation Army Store having an argument with God. And I said, "Now! What do I need with six antique Samsonite suitcases? I mean, really! I do not have enough money to fill up the car with gas. I'm not going anywhere." But it was a clear message, and I couldn't deny it. I didn't have a place to put six suitcases. But I bought them, and I took them home. And they sat there, and I looked at them, and I said, "What are you for? What are we supposed to do?"

I had been doing healing work for about a year and a half, and within a month or so after I brought home the suitcases, I began to receive invitations to travel, to go and teach about my work, to go into situations where organizations are working in crisis—sanctuary work, prisons, rape crisis centers, AIDS organizations—and to teach how a person goes into a place that looks hopeless, and makes a contribution, and blesses it, and lets it go, and goes to rest, and comes back full so he or she can do more. And how a person does this without taking on the despair of the situation.

I now have twenty suitcases, and I'm on the road about three or four months of the year. I do lots of traveling. Just about every time before I was to take a big trip, I would find a new suitcase that I was supposed to buy. The last time I bought a big suitcase was just before I met my husband, Marshall. And I thought, "Oh, I must be going on a big trip." And it certainly was.

But messages also come in ways that are not funny and even in ways that scare us. Let me tell you about one of those times for me, a time that it was very, very hard to listen. About two years ago in March, Marshall and I had just moved to Washington, D.C., from Los Angeles, and we were very happy together. After we had moved in, he said to me, "My armpits feel achy." He was thinking that maybe it was from the moving and so much lifting. Marshall didn't know anyone at that time with AIDS, but I knew that one of the first signs of AIDS is often a swelling of the lymph nodes. And I very calmly turned to him and said, "Oh, how long have they been bothering you?" "Oh, about a week." "Well, let's go see a doctor. It's important. Let's go see a doctor."

Before we got to a doctor, I sat down in prayer. No, it wasn't really prayer. I sat down in fury. I said, "How dare you. How dare you. Don't you dare threaten me like this. I go through all of these fires. I hand over my life to do this work, and you send me this love, this person who I love more than anyone else in the world. I thought we had a deal. Don't you remember that day I looked up in the sky, and I said, 'You've given me all these gifts, but you haven't sent me a lover. I think I can deal with that, but you should send more money.' I thought we had an understanding and now you're doing this? If this man is hurt, I quit the company. I'll get a new boss. I'm out of here."

I was furious. Furious. And always the message came back, "Feel this. Feel this deeply." So we went to the doctor and took the HIV antibody test. In that week it took for the results to come back, I came around to a place of saying, "All right, all right, I'm sorry I threatened you, but now I will tell you the truth. If you hurt this man, if this man suffers and you take him from me, my heart will be broken and I will not be able to do this work anymore. I cannot go out on this limb and see the suffering that I see and have people's pain pass through me because I will be so full of my own." And the message kept coming back, "Feel this deeply."

We both tested negative for the virus, and all that was needed was a little medication for a bacterial infection. And the next week I was invited to begin my work with Comadres of El Salvador to work on refugees who have been tortured. And I said, "Oh. Feel this deeply. Feel what it's like to have the person you love most in the world threatened and maybe taken away, and your own life endangered. Feel this deeply, because now I give you the opportunity to go and work with people who live with this every day, who have memory of the things that people fear most in the world, that they and the people they love most in the world will be hurt beyond all that can be imagined."

Let me sing you a song that I wrote. When I began to work with Comadres, I had a hard time finding work with refugees who had been tortured. I went to Amnesty International, and I didn't say I was a healer because I know that scares people. I said I was a massage therapist, which I am. And they sent me over to the Guatemalan Physicians Health Task Force. And they sent me over to the Hispanic Mental Health Clinic, and they sent me over to the mayor's Office on Latino Affairs. And I thought, "Well, this is not working." So I called up a good Catholic communist friend of mine, and I said, "Mary, you know what I do. Can you find me someone to work on?" She said, "Let me make a few calls." And in a day or two I was down at the office of Comadres and met a beautiful, strong, little, brown woman, Maria Tula. Her husband had been murdered. She had been abducted and tortured twice, and gang-raped by soldiers when she was seven-and-a-half months pregnant. Part of her torture was to have a knife scored along her belly with threats to take her baby from her. She later had that baby in prison.

When the international outcry arose that one of the founders of Comadres was in prison being hurt, President Duarte brought her out of prison for a press conference and said, "You can see that she is perfectly well. We have dropped all of the charges against her. We see that she is perfectly innocent, and you can see that we have democracy here in El Salvador." Maria marched up to the microphone and said, "I was tortured by this general right over here."

She made her way to the United States. She was helped across the border by Quakers. I sat down with her, and through a translator, I said, "Maria, I have a big spirit following me and sometimes when I touch people, they stop hurting, and they sleep better, and their sadness leaves them." And her eyes got very big, and I thought, "Oh, she's looking at me to see if I'm crazy." She said, "It would be very beautiful if you could make this go away. When can we start?" And we've been working for two years now. This is a song that just came out the other day as I was driving along. It's called "Maria."

### Maria

See Maria, isn't she lovely?
See her watching her children as they play.
Looking in their eyes, she sees tomorrow.
See Maria, isn't she lovely?

See Maria, strong and brave.
What the soldiers did to her, it breaks my heart to say.
Now she tells the story in all of our churches,
and the soldiers keep killing,
and we know who pays them.
Maria, Maria, Maria of El Salvador,
if they send her back,
we'll all die a little, a little, a little.

*The Dance*

I want to share one more idea with you. And really I think that of everything that I have had a chance to experience, this is the most important. For every person, for every situation, when one is looking to get well from trauma, from hurt, from some sort of serious hard time, there is a common element. It is the dance between hope and fear. And it takes place in every person who's looking to get well.

On one hand we have fear—this thing we learn as we go through life. We bump into something and are afraid that we are going to be hurt again. It's very pushy. It's very loud and aggressive. You can hear it in people's voices all the time. It's learned. It's not original equipment, but it seems very logical following hard times, following a time when you've been hurt deeply.

And on the other hand we have hope—not very well understood in our culture. We confuse hope with wishing. Hope is a very specific idea. It's a very old word. Its original definition is "the desire for goodness with the expectation that it can be achieved." That's very powerful. Everyone has hope. When a child turns to suckle, it is not committing an idle act of survival. It is revealing a desire to thrive, to be in the world. It is making an act of hope. So are children's many questions in the classroom about how the world works. Hope is a passion, and everyone has lots of it. Everyone has all they need to do the work that's in front of them.

Let me tell you one story about hope to show you how absolutely strong it is. One day I was doing massage on a fellow named Mikel. He was very ill with AIDS. He was close to dying, and he said, "Are you working on anyone else this week?" I said, "Yes, I'll be working with Sabina." "Oh, what's going on for her?" "Well, fifteen or twenty years ago someone came and stole Sabina's youngest child and murdered her. And that sadness now is in her back, and her back hurts. And when we work, she grieves that loss, and the pain goes away." And Mikel said, "Oh, my God, I could never deal with anything like that."

And later that week, I was working with Sabina, and she said, "Are you working with anyone else this week?" And I said, "Yes, I'll be working with Mary Alice." "Oh, what's going on for her?" "Well, about a year ago on one very bad morning, she was raped at knife-point, shot by a rifle, and then blown up by a bomb, all in a couple of hours." Sabina said, "Oh, my God, I could never deal with anything like that."

And then I was working with Mary Alice and she said, "Are you still helping that poor man with AIDS to die?" And I said, "Yes." And she said, "Oh, I could never deal with anything like that."

So you see, because hope is so strong, we can each of us deal with a lot of things, it's just that no one wants to volunteer. Hope is very, very strong. It's a passion, and everyone has piles of it. The problem is that it gets covered over by discouragement and pain and all these other things. But hope is very strong, and hope has a very particular job in healing.

Some sort of monster has shown up. The you-know-what has hit the fan, and now we are in trouble. We're hurting, or there's great danger, or there's some sort of trauma going down for a person or a group or for an organization or something. And Fear says, "Aha! You see? I told you there were monsters out there, and you weren't being careful, and now I'm sitting down in the driver's seat, and we're going to have some rules. We're not going out at night. We're going to sit up straight. We're going to fold our hands.

We're not going to say too much. Grrrr. I'm in charge!" And that's Fear. Pushy. Very logical. It closes all the doors and windows to protect us from a monster. It closes all the same doors and windows that our goodies come through, all the things that nourish our spirit and our bodies.

And Hope comes over and says, "Now, Fear, I understand why you're doing this. I saw the monster, too, and I know that there were damages. But, frankly you have made life so small that I am bored to tears in here. Could we open up a window? Could we draw the drapes? Could we come out from under the futon for just five minutes and stop screaming? Could we go for a walk? See a friend? Have some ice cream, a little something? I need something. We need more space in here. We need some light. We need some fresh air." And that's the job of Hope: to lobby within the legislature of the heart for space, to come over to Fear, who's trying to run the entire show, and rattle the armor, and say, "I think we can crack a window and sneak in some goodies here."

The place we see this most often is when someone close to us dies. And you have a friend, who's sort of a good friend, but not a *really* good friend, and you're telling them what happened, and you talk to them about your sadness. But it's just talking, it's just telling the story. And then you have a very good friend, someone you trust, someone whose love you find credible. He or she comes and sits with you, and you tell the same story, and the next thing you know, you are a puddle of tears, swept away by your grief. That's your hope saying, "Aha! So-and-so is in town, we can let it rip." This dance between hope and fear goes on.

That's why the nature of healing is cyclical. None of it happens all at once. There's trauma, and people do some initial work to assess the damages and see what needs doing. They make some decisions, they take some actions, and then comes around a time to rest. That rest is very important. Then comes time to do some work again, to make another assessment of the damages, take another look and see what needs doing, and then make some more decisions, take some more action.

Hope comes over just every once in a while. It doesn't do it all the time. You can't do your work all the time; it's too hard. It's too hard to do your healing work all the time. You have to rest. And the rest is just as important as the work. They go together. And that's very true for those of us who are looking to be of help to other people, as well as those of us who are looking to be of help to ourselves. And that dance between hope and fear is going on all the time, for everyone who is looking to get well. And if you watch very carefully in yourself and in your Meeting, you will see that there is a moment sometime, someplace, where hope shows up. And that's the time to give it vitamins. That's the time to encourage it with our tenderness and with our truth and honesty. Let me sing you one last song. Let me get the guitar here:

## Hello Sun

Rose looks out from her blanket,
and she wonders how she'll get through the day.
You see, Tommy died last summer,
and she's afraid she'll never laugh again.
Now she could take her own life
or stick around and see what's next.
She looks out on another new day.
She says, "Good morning, dawn,
it's so good to see you today.
Hello, Sun, it's me again.
Do you think you could come out and play?"

Tom was surrounded by shining
and he felt himself drifting away.
The moment he died, a journey began
and he wonders if he'll come round this way.
Now he'll miss this old world
but that body was hell.
He looks into the light, and he says,
he says, "Good morning, dawn,
it's so good to see you today.
Hello, Sun, it's me again.
Do you think you could come out and play?"

Carlos looks out from the old car he's been sleeping in,
and he smiles just to be alive.
He's lost everything but a little joie de vivre
that he keeps in what's left of his mind.
Now he and the sun have come round again.
He looks out at his old friend and says,
he says, "Good morning, dawn,
it's so good to see you today.
Hello, Sun, it's me again.
Do you think you could come out and play?"

Every morning around the world,
as life begins again,
and the joy and the pain
and the beauty and the sorrow
come swirling 'round everyone's way.
Oh, what will you say when tomorrow comes around,
and what did you say today?
You say, "Good morning, dawn,
it's so good to see you today.
Hello, Sun, it's me again.
Do you think you could come out and play?"

I am so grateful to be with you this week. I am so grateful to all the many people who work so hard to bring this Gathering together, who work for years for each Gathering. I'm so grateful to the people who brought the Names Project AIDS Memorial Quilt to FGC this year. If you haven't seen it yet, don't miss it. It is stunning. I'm so grateful to all the people who made it possible to bring it here, especially John Meyer and Lyle Jenks.

The prayer that I opened with is the prayer that I use every time I do some work on someone. And when I finish a piece of work, I stand back and I say:

*Dear Great and Holy Spirit, please wash me. Thank you for this opportunity for loving, and please keep me ready for more.*

# A Little Gracefulness

John Calvi

STUFF    STUFF    STUFF    TO FEEL WHEN WAY

O-PENS TAKES A LIT-TLE GRACE-FUL-NESS I BE-LIEVE THERE'S PLEN-TY I BE-

LIEVE    THAT YOU CARE    I BE-LIEVE IN ME AND THE

SUN THAT'S AL-WAYS SHIN - ING SOME-WHERE

TAKES A LIT-TLE QUI-ET. OO    TAKES A LIT-TLE

JOY    JOY    JOY TAKES SOME BE-LIEV-ING    IN    GOOD

VERY SLOW    RIT.

SOME-TIMES    I RE-MEM-BER

# CARRY AND BURN
## (CLAUDE'S SONG)

JOHN CALVI

CAR - RY AND BURN. CAR - RY AND BURN

THIS FIRE-WOOD I GATH - ER TO CAR - RY AND

BURN, AND MY LOVE IS THE SAME OH MY

LOVE IS THE SAME WE GATH - ER AND GATH - ER TO

CAR - RY AND BURN. I'M AF - RAID OF THE FI-

RE IT WILL CHANGE ME I KNOW.

WHAT WILL BE LEFT WHEN I PASS

THROUGH OF THE ME I KNOW NOW WHAT WILL BE

The Dance Between Hope & Fear

NOW LIKE AN-Y LOVE IT UN - DRES-SES YOU.

AND GIVES TOO MUCH. AND ASKS MORE

THAN YOU HAVE. AND THE VIEW FROM

HERE AND THE VIEW FROM HERE IS

MORE MORE THAN ONE CHOOS - ES.

The Dance Between Hope & Fear

# MARIA

John Calvi

2

KIL-LING    AND  WE KNOW  WHO PAYS THEM        MA-

RI - A   MA - RI - A   MA - RI - A  OF  EL  SAL - VA - DOR   IF THEY

MORENDO

SEND  HER  BACK   WE'LL  ALL   DIE    A   LIT - TLE        A

LIT - TLE         A   LIT - LE_____

# Hello Sun

John Calvi

1. ROSE LOOKS OUT FROM HER BLANKET AND SHE WON-DERS HOW SHE'LL GET THROUGH THE DAY YOU SEE TOMMY DIED LAST SUMMER SHE'S AFRAID SHE'LL NEV-ER LAUGH A-GAIN NOW SHE COULD TAKE HER OWN LIFE OR STICK A-ROUND AND SEE WHAT'S NEXT SHE LOOKS OUT AT AN-OTH-ER NEW DAY AND SHE SAYS GOOD MORN - ING DAWN IT'S SO

2. TOM WAS SUR-ROUN-DED BY SHIN-NING AND HE FELT HIM - SELF SLIP-PING A-WAY THE MOM - ENT HE DIED A JOUR-NEY BE-GAN AND HE WON-DERS IF HE'LL COME 'ROUND THIS WAY NOW HE'LL MISS THIS OLD WORLD BUT THAT BO - DY WAS HELL HE LOOKS IN - TO THE LIGHT AND HE SAYS HE SAYS GOOD

CHORUS

The Dance Between Hope & Fear

The Dance Between Hope & Fear

The Dance Between Hope & Fear

# Section 2

# Early Years

Teaching                            27

The Ones Who Aren't Here            31

Fool's Service                      38

Courage                             40

Naming the Beethoven Letter         42

Coming to Washington                43

Going to Pendle Hill                45

My Spiritual Blessing               52

# Teaching

*April 20, 2013*

I've always been a teacher. I can remember helping young cousins learn to skate and swim. I taught swimming as a teenager at a summer camp and later on taught guitar, banjo, and dulcimer at another camp.

I became a good teacher while learning the Montessori method at the Whitby School in Greenwich, Connecticut, and while teaching music summers at Camp Killooleet in Hancock, Vermont. I learned the first work of careful observation and preparation—*pre*paration, the work one does before the work so it goes smoothly.

I learned the balance of kindness and structure to welcome each student and corral squirrely attention. At first I enjoyed the easy kids who responded well to simple guidance. Later I became intrigued by the kids who didn't fit the usual patterns and needed something extra to settle in. My best teachers helped me to see into their lives. I learned to help these kids understand their own needs and sense the needs of others. And so my healing gift began as I learned how to read a child and feel the child's essence, especially his or her needs.

I worked with children three to six in Montessori schools for eight years, and in summer camps for thirteen years. This included the years that I was becoming a musician and storyteller, performing as soon as I was able. I learned to show my authentic self clearly to set the tone of my work so others would show their authentic selves.

I learned careful observation and that children are our emotional equals from Rosa Packard in Greenwich. John and Ellie Seeger of Killooleet showed me how a whole and authentic teacher brings out honesty and integrity in others.

I was not a good academic teacher. I was much more interested in seeing that each child had what he or she needed to unfold to their best self. This fit very neatly with learning so that obstacles were removed and the students pursued what interested them. Creating a classroom for two dozen children, who don't need the teacher much because they are using the classroom as it was designed, is a triumph. I had lots of that in the latter part of my classroom years. Setting up a beautiful room full of interesting things was a joy . . . and *tons* of work.

My gift seemed to be setting up the culture in a classroom where students felt welcomed, learned choice, and sought what interested them—never mind that the deck was stacked because there were no "toys" from popular culture to starve their minds.

At first I thought I would do this forever. Create my own school, set a tone of respect with everyone realizing that children are our emotional equals. I was still thinking along the lines of what I could give to make change. I hadn't realized that the changes were taking place in me as I learned this work.

Teaching children taught me discipline, compassion, and pragmatic giving as responses to myself and the world. I didn't realize it was the beginning of my own healing and preparation for larger work. I often found these principles were integrated within me during the silence of Quaker Meeting.

~

After about a decade I needed a change. I had no college and had graduated high school with minimal grades. I wanted with all my heart the luxury of being in school for my own seeking, without being in service to others. I left teaching for massage school with some sense of wanting to work deeper, and yet also wanting to escape the flood of needs that a roomful of children and their parents bring each day. I even had some thoughts of winding up on a cruise ship doing massage among lovely tropic islands surrounded by plenty. However, in the back of my mind I had begun to hear voices and to wonder about their directives to me. Hearing voices did seem a bit odd, but I also had family stories of spiritual experiences and beliefs that made it easy to accept possible unknown paths.

I entered massage school thinking I was choosing a new path, not knowing what that path might be. I was thirty and had spent my whole life underweight with the curved posture of a whipped dog. As school proceeded, numerous emotional issues came forward, and I dealt with them in classes, in therapy, and with colleagues.

A huge leap took place in a class of massage for the release of deep emotion. This class scared most students, but I was fascinated with the power and transformation that takes place when some old stuff stuck in the body is squeezed out and pushed into Light for cleansing and understanding.

The teacher, the amazing Tirza Firestone, now author and rabbi, reached deep into my gut with a fist, pushed hard and slow, asking me for words. The entire class watched my process. Finally after much sweat and fearful tears came a very young voice saying, "Don't hit me." The years of living in my father's house and enduring not only the violence but the constant threat of violence had shaped my body, mind, and emotional life like a prisoner held in constant restraints. I was a late bloomer in part because I was working very hard to remain numb.

Another marvelous teacher, Linda Krier, taught a class in how to "read" posture and working with what could be seen in addition to what a client might say. The way we hold ourselves and how we might shift an old posture are pivotal points of change.

Before long my body began to change. My posture became more upright. I was taller. I was no longer underweight, which I realize had been a sign that I never felt safe. Rather, I developed muscles and coordination of graceful movement for the first time in my life. I looked and felt like a different person, a much better, happier person. I had a confidence and a delight in the world that was freeing and made me eager to know the world as this new self.

It was about this time that I began to work with women rape survivors. I moved into the new work as the old teacher I'd become: carrying with me good welcome, a safe environment, careful observation, and respectful connection. I thought I was bringing simple compassion—a good person offering a kindness. But my hands kept getting warm, and young women who thought they might never relax again felt deep relaxation, safety, and trust. The resulting transaction was the same as in my classroom, but this was a much more deeply intimate work with very wounded people.

Soon I would begin similar work with people with AIDS, and again my hands became very warm. People lost their fear, relaxed deeply, and had the calm needed to choose their next decisions and actions. People who never expected to breathe again without being overwhelmed by anxiety felt great relief and calm. What I could offer was peace in the midst of huge life wounds. This taught that peace still existed and was within reach. There were ways to find it. This was as important as teaching reading and writing, but it involved more trust and hence got me more stoned (high) with each work. There was no sense that my gift was to change tissue or disease, but rather to release pain.

The work with rape and AIDS brought me great excitement, but also great fatigue, some depression, and even illness. How could one be with all this tragedy, feel it deeply, and get clean and refreshed to do more?

~

I began an involuntary study of burnout over the years. As I learned disciplines of rest and cleansing, I taught these to others. Whether I was learning about how to work with early childhood sexual abuse in an adult body or ways to work with a very new disease that had neither a name yet nor a known cause, the teacher in me was always thinking: "I need to demonstrate this; it might help more people."

Later on, when I was working with prison inmates, tortured refugees, ritual abuse survivors—I wanted to help all these dear people. But always these experiences were also studies in what I already knew and what more I could learn. Much of my learning in each instance came from guidance. I receive messages like someone is whispering in my ear. But it's not really words and it's not really sound, but rather thoughts being given me from somewhere beyond myself, way beyond what I learned in anatomy, physiology, and pathology classes.

And so along with working with trauma survivors of all manner of hurt and teaching ways to avoid burnout for caregivers, I also teach massage, energy work, and meditations for cleansing. All this needs to be familiar and used by more people. Much good needs to be carried out as the world is in tough shape and people seem to learn the lessons of kindness in very spotty ways indeed.

One thing that has always drawn me to teaching is the trust involved. We must have some amount of trust to learn from another person. I love feeling that other persons place trust in me. And the more important the teaching, the deeper the trust that is required. There is no deep learning without trust. To feel trustworthy is also a humbling and joyful confirmation and another part of the give and take in wonder and learning that I enjoy. Trust depends on the hospitality of the teacher and the seeking of the student working together.

# The Ones Who Aren't Here

Some songs have so much history in the songwriter's life, it's like telling the story of one's own childhood. This song trails through many parts of my life, in the deepest ways.

I left home at eighteen, but was thrown out of my family at the age of twenty-nine, told to never come home again because I was gay. Now, my immediate family was not such a bad one to be thrown out of. There was alcoholism, violence, knives, guns, state police, gambling, whoring, and mafia wannabes, all in that little house of five people. Gay shouldn't have even made the front page let alone the headlines.

I had a long winter of depression.

With the help of excellent massage therapy, the depression lifted with the writing of this song on an early spring day. I had begun to sing at gay coffeehouses around New England. I realized that the work of coming out was so scary and so dangerous that for every person I was singing to, hundreds of thousands more were hiding at home, never to feel the warmth of a community without secrets.

I wrote the song in 1981 on a Vermont Spring day, with melting snow, bright sunshine, and a hint that winter was finally over once again, a day of relief and promise. As the tune came to me, the words came naturally. I wrote it out on brown paper with a big fat pencil. It came all at once with no editing, no pushing to fit or hard-to-find words, a natural childbirth. And when it was done, I couldn't stop singing it, maybe twenty or thirty times. I just couldn't stop, and my deep inner sadness left as though scoured by vibration. It had what I admired in Pete Seeger's writing: it added up the troubles and then named the hopeful parts. It had the poetry I admired in Joni Mitchell's work though the tune was simpler. The contentment of making this song ran all through me.

I wanted to give it to one of my favorite singer/songwriters, Meg Christian. She was the first gay performer I'd ever heard. I wrapped up a tape with a note for her and tried to go backstage to see her at a concert in Northampton, Massachusetts. Two large bouncers stopped me at the stage door like Secret Service women guarding the president, but they did deliver the gift. More than a year later, Meg sent a postcard to thank me, and I heard through the grapevine that she was using "Ones" in concerts.

Six months later, I had left my work as a Montessori teacher with young children in Vermont. I was in my first semester at the

Boulder School of Massage in Colorado about to take my first anatomy exam. I have never been a good student. My learning disabilities are vast, defined late in life, and accentuated by stress. Just as we were to begin the exam, in comes my friend and fellow student Mig to say she had just come from New York City where she heard Meg Christian sing my song at Carnegie Hall and mention my name to the standing ovation, sellout crowd. I must have passed the exam, but oh!—the trials of concentration that night.

The very good news was that soon after the Carnegie Hall concert recording was released, I had begun my AIDS work. The royalties from the first year gave me enough money to buy a professional quality massage table and continue my work. This is the table that I have used to work with people with AIDS, sexually assaulted women and men, tortured refugees, inmates, and addicts since 1983.

A second and very beautiful recording of the song was made in 1988 by Suede for her first album, *Easily Suede*. By then, my husband, Marshall Brewer, and I had moved to Washington, D.C., where Suede was recording. She came to borrow my Martin guitar to record "Ones" and did a beautiful, soulful version.

~

"The Ones Who Aren't Here" has been performed by gay and lesbian choruses around the world. It's been used at weddings and memorials, radio shows, plays, and gay pride marches throughout North America. One never knows when the child goes out into the world how this child will be received or how far it will travel and be heard. I am so happy that this song has met such a great welcome in the world and continues to move great crowds each year.

## The Ones Who Aren't Here

I'm thinking about the ones who aren't here
and won't be coming in late.
Home all alone and the family
and won't be coming out tonight.
Wish I could know all the lovers and friends
kept from gathering
I think of you now, the ways you could go,
we're all of us refugees.

Telling myself and the family,
my friends and the folks on the job.
One by one, and it's never been easy,
and me and everyone changed.
The hugs and the tears when they show you their heart,
and some never speak again.
Every pot off the wheel can't bear the kiln,
and every love can't bear the pain.

So let's pass a kiss and a happy sad tear
and a hug the whole circle round.
For the ones who aren't here, for the hate and the fear,
for laughter, for struggle, for life.
Let's have a song here for me and for you
and the love we cannot hide.
Let's have a song for the ones who aren't here,
and won't be comin' out tonight.

# The Ones Who Aren't Here

John Calvi

I'M THINK-ING A-BOUT THE ONES WHO AREN'T HERE

AND WON'T BE COM-ING IN LATE.

HOME ALL A - LONE AND THE FAM - I - LY

AND WON'T BE COM-ING OUT TO - NIGHT.

WISH I COULD KNOW ALL THE LOV - ERS AND FRIENDS

KEPT FROM GATH-ER - ING

I THINK OF YOU NOW

THE WAYS YOU COULD GO. WE'RE ALL OF US

Early Years

CAN'T BEAR THE KILN AND EV-ERY LOVE

CAN'T BEAR THE PAIN.___

SO LET'S PASS A KISS___ AND A HAP-PY SAD___

TEAR AND A HUG THE WHOLE CIR-CLE 'ROUND.___

— FOR THE ONES WHO AREN'T HERE___ FOR THE HATE AND THE FEAR

FOR LAUGH-TER FOR STRUG-GLE___ FOR LIFE.___

— LET'S HAVE A SONG___ HERE FOR ME AND FOR

YOU AND THE LOVE THAT WE CAN-NOT HIDE_____

Early Years

AND LET'S HAVE A SONG FOR THE ONES WHO AREN'T HERE____ AND WON'T BE COM-IN' OUT TO - NIGHT____

# Fool's Service

It hasn't been easy to make all the mistakes I have made. It's taken a special kind of whatever the opposite of attention and concentration is. At times I excel in this. It's not everyone who can trip over a flat space. There's a certain skill to it. And it's very underappreciated. Think of what a public service it is to relieve others of their fear of doing something embarrassing because center stage has been stolen by the guy with the toilet paper stuck to the bottom of his shoe while he discusses the importance of making a good first impression.

There was the time I decided to show off how brave I was climbing up onto the horse without a saddle or bridle to go for a ride. I was ten and this horse had never been ridden. It was a very short ride. She took off at a gallop, which was fine until she came to the fence and took a sharp corner. I tended to go forward in mid-air.

There was the time I climbed up to ride the pregnant cow. Her back was so broad and wide that my legs lay completely straight. So when the cow bucked she only had to do it once. My riding days were over early.

There was the time I took a job teaching archery. I knew less than nothing about archery. I shot twice at summer camp when I was nine. My arrows never even considered going near the target. And here I was with three days to practice before the kids arrived and I had to teach. I did learn how to hit the target. I practiced until my fingers throbbed with mediocre success. When the kids got there I never shot. I borrowed a very large deadly *deadly* hunting bow, which I hung near all the little kid bows. As they reached for their bows each morning and saw this Robin Hood machine, I was assumed to be Dead Eye John of the archery range.

I taught everything the little booklet said was important. And they learned how to do it. Everybody got better. Seems I did know how to teach even if I didn't know how to shoot. There was a teenager who had won several competitions and asked to shoot with me in a private session one afternoon. He said he wanted tips, but I think he wanted to see me shoot and beat my score. That afternoon we moved far back from the targets. He shot first. He got one bulls-eye and the other four arrows in the next circle. He stood aside, quite pleased with himself. On the outside I was cool. Inside, I was yelling at myself. How could I be so stupid to take this job? Why did I lie and say sure I could teach this, no problem.

I took my stance and raised my killer bow. I don't know what prayers I said, but I shot five bulls-eyes and never had to shoot again all summer. By supper time and for several years later, I was famous for shooting nothing but bulls-eyes.

# Courage

*May 1999*

I tied the knot tightly, a bola-on-coil, around her waist and eased her to the edge of the cliff. I turned to the other teenagers and said, "Here's something you can use all your life. Courage is not about never being afraid. It's really about knowing you're afraid and going on. Not knowing how and making your own way."

Later on, I was having to come up with more about courage than I knew. I had chosen a path that would show me things that I couldn't bear on my own. Should I look without seeing? Was it possible to know these pains in my mind without letting my heart feel them?

I was teaching about AIDS in a prison. The prison doctor took us on a tour of the facilities. The few prisoners with AIDS had over-flowed into a locked psychiatric ward. Not only were they surrounded by madness; they were also told they had a new disease and that no one knew how to help, not the local hospital and no one on staff at the prison. What I recall most were the eyes of one man. He sat on his hospital bed in his small cell. His eyes held the kind of loneliness of one set adrift, totally separate, without maps or steering, never to land again at anything known. He had too much illness for any real tension. His fear and grief fought for his attention, and his body remained floating, waiting. I saw the yellow surrounding the brown eyes, his gaze returning mine, no words, just the knowing that he watched me seeing him alone where he wouldn't be reached, ever.

So courage took on a new aspect of surrender, to surround myself in the cloak of prayer or reverence and seek guidance. And by and by, I felt surrounded by Light and purpose and hope that grew and shined. Courage now included a clearer sense of purpose, of not being alone, and of not mistaking myself as the source of what was being offered. And, finally, not allowing the impossible to dissuade me by fear or distraction.

Still there were times when I was being shown too much, and it threatened to break my heart, rob me of all sense of beauty or justice in things, and dim my compass through the fog of doubt and the pain of others.

I recall a young boy with AIDS at the weekend retreat saying that his doctor would test his brain for infection on Monday. Saturday and Sunday, he lost more motor control until he knew that walking would be impossible soon, very soon. We were on the stairs together, stumbling on our way to the massage table, when the look in his eye told me he could see the future of next week, and next month, as he lost his freedom of movement. How could my eyes see his terror, feel his grief, and go on?

There was a young girl who screamed sometimes about what they had done to her when she was very young. Her panic made the past time of her wounds immediate. She lost track of today and got lost in the pain of events twenty years ago. She screamed stories that hurt to hear. And I couldn't reach where she was until she got tired out, and by then I'd heard too much. Was it courage to just stay until she grew weary? At one retreat she sat opposite me at dinner. A therapist rose and made an announcement about fundraising for victims of the rape camps in Bosnia. This young girl heard the words "rape camp" and she began to leave somewhere in her mind. It was by my eyes and my hands reaching hers that I said, "You are here with me now and we are not in danger." It was reaching over the panic to her need for help that made me feel strong enough to have courage, courage enough for her until she grew to have her own.

Courage these days seems to be holding on to what I know. When doubt comes to unsettle, when pain interrupts my vision and spiritual guidance, when all I know from these years of seeking slips into fog—courage seems to be simply knowing that the fog passes. Knowing the Light returns. Knowing spring comes after winter. Courage is not being without fear so much as it is finding a place for the fear that will not interrupt going forward.

# Naming the Beethoven Letter

I have been living on gifts for thirty years, and every year I send out a Beethoven Letter. The letter got its name in a "Marx Brothers see the Light" kind of way. I was in the middle of a certification program at the Boulder School of Massage Therapy in Colorado. Along with teaching great massage, the school was teaching the importance of resumes and business cards and business plans. It was the fall of 1983. It was not widely known that the terrible new disease, to be named AIDS, was related to a virus passed with sex. We didn't understand the disease. We didn't have medicines. Healthcare providers were scared to touch people with AIDS, as were families, lovers, and friends. I told the health department I'd give massage to people with AIDS anywhere in the state whether or not they could pay.

Soon I was graduated, but I couldn't get spa work because everyone knew about the AIDS work I was doing. They were afraid of what might be under my fingernails. I had work but no one to pay me since many of the men I worked on at that time had no resources. So much for a business plan.

AIDS didn't make it onto a disability list for quite a while so people had to go broke before there was any help. The Surgeon General, under orders, didn't mention it for years!

Six months after I began the work, I wrote a letter to 100 friends saying, "I am doing something beautiful. Who will help me?" Half of them wrote back saying, "I will!"

A dear friend and colleague mentioned to me that Beethoven did a similar thing. He had very little money in his later years, but friends kept him composing by giving him gifts. That was the beginning of my living on gifts.

# Coming to Washington

*A letter to "Dear Friends"*
*Washington, D.C., October 17, 1988*

I have been meaning to write to you for some time. The days fill up, and I keep thinking I must remember to tell about this day, or that moment, and suddenly the next is upon me.

I have been home with Marshall for about six weeks. While I was gone all of August teaching through New England, he moved us into a basement apartment and began to unpack sixty boxes and twenty suitcases. I was very tired when I returned and I spent a week napping, discovering the contents of suitcases seven through twenty, and having contact only with Marshall. It was a much needed luxury.

As our home gets pulled together with—

"Where shall we put the table cloths?"

"How about we put them back in the suitcase until we find a table?"

We get a call—

"Hello, this is Mary from Friends Meeting of Washington, and I have an old oak table that I was wondering if you could use."

So it all got pulled together in amazing ways.

My second week back I began to see clients and write the follow-up and thank you letters to the individuals and organizations I had seen in August. And began to answer the fifty pieces of mail that had collected in the meantime. And began to address the inquiries about future teaching dates. I now have at least one teaching or singing engagement per month for the next year. One fellow I saw was very near dying, though he had been quite hearty before I left:

"Greg, what are you doing? You told me you were just going to stick around while it was fun?"

"Yes, well, my family is taking good care of me, so I guess I am not ready yet."

His family is in the next room relieved that I am a professional that they do not have to help. They do not want to watch. They don't touch him. They wash after they touch anything he has touched. It is clear they love him deeply, but in this setting they don't know how. The cancer has so disfigured him and made his breathing so difficult that not holding him or even touching his hand hurts them almost as much as the thought of touching him. They are very jealous of the nurse, a good friend, a former lover, and of me . . . because we touch in love and without fear. As a result the family finds something wrong with each of us. I only got to work on him three times, and then he died in the middle of the night in the arms of his best friend and the old lover. It was peaceful.

I also went back to Comadres where both Maria Tula and America Sousa have been on tour to many churches in many states. Both of them are well considering how their lives have been skewed in such dramatic ways. Maria presents me with a recommendation letter, which I enclose, and it makes me teary to hear how she expresses her gratitude to me. She shows me a poster of her latest tour.

"It's beautiful," I say. "You're famous!"
She smiles and says, "Ya."

I try to think if I know the Italian word for famous so I can try it in quasi-Spanish, because I know she has not understood what I have said other than to know I am happy for her.

# Going to Pendle Hill

*A letter to "Dear Friends"*
*August 1990*

I am very sorry to be so out of touch. I am usually much better at not having letters build up. But I am now, to my great embarrassment, six months behind. I have wonderful letters from March that have sat at the bottom of the stacks, and the stacks have grown and grown. Apparently, a bit too much has been going on, and now I am sitting down to write a long letter and send it out with thanks for being in touch. With apologies for not writing sooner. And with a few stories.

In February, Marshall and I visited Pendle Hill, a Quaker center for contemplation and study west of Philadelphia. We were guests of the friend I'd met while teaching. We'd been invited to rest. I did some work with two residents who were very tired from their jobs in the AIDS epidemic. While I was helping one with her extreme fatigue, Marshall and our good friend, Muriel Bishop, sat in the library. They simultaneously hit upon the idea that I should be at Pendle Hill for spring term, March 30 to June 9. They decided I needed a good long rest. They also thought I wouldn't agree to come to Pendle Hill to rest, but I might agree to come to work on my book. The idea was a shock. It seemed at once beautiful and too luxurious. It took me a week of consideration and much encouragement to apply. And then I had one month to take care of finding funds, the task of stepping out of an overly busy life, meeting with clients and arranging calendars, plus organizing my thoughts and packing luggage for a time of quiet.

Before leaving Washington, D.C., I helped a friend to die in hospital. He had told me the previous week that he could feel his body was in rapid decline and if the doctors did not intervene he would die soon. There was no visible sign of this, but I could sense his words were quite true, and as I proceeded with our usual energy work, it only seemed more true. He relaxed deeply and got close to sleep, which was a real gift considering his previous agitation. As I left his room I was not sure I would see Mark again.

Denny, Mark's best friend, and I arrived a week later. Mark's kidneys had stopped working altogether, and true to his wishes, he was not hooked up to a machine to prolong his life. He was on morphine for the pain and being allowed to die as comfortably as possible. His decline had been rapid and about as ugly as it gets. He was unable to talk, see, or swallow. He was tied to his bed and through moans and thrashing made it clear he was terrified. All of my gifts were brought to bear as I rolled up my sleeves to help one friend with my hands while talking to the other friend, who was stunned at the horror show of disease. If I have worked harder or in more complicated situations I do not recall them. We gave him what comfort we could with massage, energy work, and conversation. He recognized me and allowed me to calm him. As Denny took in this horrendous sight of a loved one, he moved from overwhelming grief to competent caregiving. He returned later that evening with others, and Mark died surrounded by good care.

I worked with other clients as I prepared for departure. Then two weeks before leaving for Pendle Hill I got a call from Keith, a dear friend in St. Paul, asking me to come there and help him die.

Oh dear. I was exhausted, but I had promised him I would be there when he was ready. Of the many people I have helped to die of AIDS since beginning seven years ago, this was the dearest friend. I wanted to do this, and I knew I did not have enough energy. I told him I wanted to talk it over with Marshall and find a cheap flight. Marshall and I decided I could so long as I was back in time for spring term. This meant probably not staying until Keith died. I searched for a cheap flight and none could be found. As I was about to give up, Louise called offering me her frequent flyer ticket to be with Keith. So I called him, and it was all arranged. But the express mail envelope went to neighbors instead of me, and through carelessness my airline ticket ended up in their garbage, where I found it two days after the flight left, without me. The intensity and number of emotions I felt are impossible to name here. But I can safely say it was all too much. Keith died peacefully five weeks later surrounded by much love and care.

I arrived at Pendle Hill the end of March with great weariness, relief, and expectations. And too many suitcases full of too many projects. I had new songs to copyright, correspondence to catch up on, business records to update, rope to crochet a hammock, books to read, an upcoming summer tour to prepare for, a book to write, and workshops to design. I had been cautioned from all sides that Pendle Hill is full of interesting people doing wonderful things, and it would be nearly impossible to rest and focus on a book unless I was very careful. So I set out straight away to make myself a hermitage. I introduced myself as a Quaker healer tired from work in the epidemic and with tortured refugees, and had come to rest, and as that happened I would be working on a book about healing from trauma. What I really needed was a Quaker monastery, but I fashioned that fairly well out of the structure there.

I knew a few people and got to know a few more, but for the most part I stayed away from group gatherings. In part because I am painfully shy. But also because I needed this time to empty myself from being overfull, from seeing and feeling too much. This was an interesting aspect that held my attention and which I will attempt to explain.

When I began to travel and teach about healing, it was not unusual to come into a room full of people and notice a few scattered about the room whose pain I had some sense of. Following a lecture, workshop, or concert, often these people would seek me out. My sense of their condition usually increased and, sometimes while speaking with them, I would feel an overwhelming tenderness. I would see in them a young child regardless of their real age and feel a great care for them. By and by I understood that this was a sign from my angels that I was to work with this person and their hurt could be released. As I settled in to Pendle Hill, I noticed that my "radar" was firmly in place, but I never felt the tenderness cue to offer work. So I decided not to work on anyone until that cue returned.

Since I accepted my blessing to do healing work back in 1983, I have been very busy, mostly learning while on the job and slowly understanding the limits, boundaries, and protocols. This was my first chance to set the work and the title of HEALER aside, and get an overview of myself and my experiences. (This seems to me a lush and crucial opportunity for anyone doing important work for themselves or others.) The view backward was amazing to me. I read old journals and letters. I reviewed the previous twelve months and realized I couldn't recall who had died in which month or which state I was in. I wept and laughed and gave my first days there over to emptying myself and coming back to center.

Something that really shocked me at first was how much I slept. During the first week I began to sleep full eight and nine hours a night of deep sleep. On top of that I often caught a morning and then an afternoon nap—bringing me up to as much as fifteen hours a day of sleep. At first I thought it was wonderful. But by the second week I began to feel it was decadent. By the third week I began to wonder if I needed blood tests! And then suddenly I didn't need to sleep so much. I had more energy and a great deal more time to use it.

It was about this time that a series of nightmares came to me. And it became clear that much of my tiredness, if not most of it, had to do with recovering memories of early childhood sexual assault. The work of retrieving and deeply feeling old wounds amidst my other tasks took its toll on me in many ways. Now I had the time for some clarity and taking care of the child within me. I got some excellent help from a therapist on staff, though struggled with the fact that I am at the beginning of this work and too well defended to get as far as I want. This piece of my time at Pendle Hill was important in helping me gain a greater understanding of myself—both my gifts and my needs.

In the afternoons and evenings, I would walk with two close friends in the woods surrounding Pendle Hill. One was nearly seventy years old and the other was in the mid-seventies. We shared life stories and enjoyed the quiet of the woods, watched for rabbits, and delighted in each other's company. This was a good balance to the intense inner dialogue that involved me day and night. On one hand I needed to feel the calm pace and overview that only age can provide, and on the other it was refreshing to see how life is hard in similar ways for all ages. Mostly it was good to walk slowly and listen and watch carefully.

The work on my book began after I discovered throwing porcelain on the potter's wheel and before going to Toronto for some work. I had a book outline that I'd been fleshing out. I had great resistance to this work but also great eagerness. As a dyslexic who has read very little of the world's books and as someone who never reads for information, it had not really occurred to me what a large task doing a book is. Fortunately, writer friends have been very encouraging and have helped a good deal to boost my patience.

I set out on this idea of putting what I have been teaching in workshops about healing from trauma into a book maybe five years ago. At first it seemed hard, because each idea seems connected to every other idea, and a book needs a more linear form. Slowly it is taking shape. I have given up predicting a date for the completion of the first draft, but the book itself seems clearer and clearer to me all the time. The parts and sequence and tone are set, and each piece of writing, though going much too slowly, brings it all closer.

After discovering complete fascination with the potter's wheel and the sensuousness of porcelain, I put in some time making bowls. I had in mind to make a set of china, but almost everything I made came out looking like a dog dish. I developed symmetry, but height and thinness eluded me. Most of all I loved the feel and the process.

In the first part of May I drove to Toronto, where I had two days of work. I was a bit nervous to be back at work after a month of no work. I was afraid I'd find out I still hadn't had enough rest, but all went very well. I spent a day at Nancy Pocock's home again doing energy work on the many refugees who come there seeking the help of the Refugee Committee of Toronto Monthly Meeting. It was wonderful to be back. Nancy and her helpers get much good done there. Most of the people I worked on were men from Central America. I have been there enough that my work is somewhat known, and several came forward for work. Later I had a chance to receive some body work from Marianna Hartsong, and this was a great help in coping with the tension that built up in me as I dealt with my own healing.

The next day I taught a full day workshop on working in crisis and avoiding burnout to a group of twenty-five or thirty people working in various ways with refugees. My ideas were much appreciated. In the second half of the day I was asked to do some hands-on work for people who needed it. So the last hour of the workshop was a Meeting for Healing. We sat in a circle in the Meeting room with my massage table and a chair in the middle, and anyone who wanted could come forward for touch. The hour was filled with people coming forward. Two were Africans, one tortured under Idi Amin. A great calm surrounded us, and their tiredness was less. I think some of the depression and despair of those who had been tortured was released. I started back to Pendle Hill after supper with Elaine, and later that night I learned that Keith had died in the early evening as I crossed the border.

The second month at Pendle Hill went faster than the first. More writing, throwing pots, wrote some new music, and began to work on people again. I was able to help some friends over the phone. One friend called very teary requesting advice on helping her brother to die. The cancer was taking him quickly. How could she help him and his wife and kids, plus deal with her own grief. We spoke for half an hour, and she began to see what she could do and what she might expect. A week later she called to say it was a beautiful death. Her sadness had been joined by peace and competence.

I began to work on people at Pendle Hill before leaving. My energy had been fully restored, and I began to carefully gear up for a full summer of touring. It felt very good to be working again. The joy of it, the sense of surrounding grace, and a deeper calm.

On June 6 I headed for Ohio where I taught for two days at the first national conference on living in recovery from AIDS. I went with a friend who had recently tested positive for HIV. The adjustment to this news is difficult as you can imagine. He is a therapist specializing in addictions who has changed many people's lives. This was his first AIDS conference being primarily a receiver. We had some good talks which I think eased this difficult period for him. My teaching went well, and I worked on a few people in my room. I taught massage and anti-burnout workshops. It was a good conference with four full days of sharing and reaching for new ground, and many long-term survivors.

Next was the Friends World Committee for Consultation (FWCC). I shared some of my insights about remaining faithful to a calling during times of doubt. We also had a Meeting for Healing that was very gathered with a deep silence.

The third national conference on massage for AIDS was postponed, which gave me some time to see clients in DC. Marshall and I then spent a week in Bennington, where he worked on his master's thesis and I got some writing done too.

Then it was off to Friends General Conference (FGC) in Minnesota. I did some work on people in my room, but most of the time that week went to organizing and staffing emotional support people during the display of the NAMES Project—AIDS Memorial Quilt. Some of the highest spiritual moments of the Gathering occurred working with the quilt project. I gave the closing keynote on Friday night. I have spoken to large crowds before, but this was a very special honor. My message was well received. I haven't been that scared in a long time, but I was able to talk about some deep feelings and sing a few songs. The silence following this was very deep.

After a couple of weeks in D.C. to do laundry, unclog my desk, see clients, and pack, I was back on the road for a month. I did some work in Vermont, and then went to Maine for a gay men's conference, where I worked on several people, did a concert, a grieving circle, and two workshops. It was a great week of community.

As I write this, Marshall and I have been enjoying a week in Vermont. Marshall has been putting the final touches on his master's work, and I am getting ready for the upcoming work and catching up on desk work. From here I'll teach at New England Yearly Meeting, then September 7 to 9 I'll teach a weekend of massage for trauma at Powell House in Old Chatham, New York. In mid-September I will go to Colorado to teach and hopefully also teach in Kansas City and Cincinnati. October 12 to 14 I teach at Pendle Hill, and the Saturday after Thanksgiving I sing at the Camp Killooleet concert in New York City with Pete Seeger and the Short Sisters.

I hope you can see much has been going on. I am not getting to all of the things that I can see need getting to. But I have a list somewhere of what needs doing. I am busier than I used to be. My network of what I am asked to do and where is getting larger. So I am sorry about not writing sooner. It was on the list.

I hope this finds you well, and that I'll hear from you. Just as I close, another beautiful Vermont day is setting aside its rain clouds and beckoning wild flowers with brilliant summer sun. It's a wonderful moment and I'm glad I had a chance to see it.

# My Spiritual Blessing

*April 23, 1999*

Sometimes I receive messages about the nature of someone's pain, where the pain is in the body, how it got there, what if feels like, and how it might be removed or released.

Sometimes I recognize complete strangers and am awash with a deep tenderness for their pain, as though I have found a long lost child of my own that I am terribly happy to surround now with comfort and care.

Sometimes I can feel their pain move out of them and through me and out. It draws tears to my eyes, feels like it's going to tear me open. If I just surrender and stay in the Light, it washes through but tires me.

Sometimes I surrender to the Light leading me on, and I feel myself becoming my best self and more than myself. When the work is over I feel a retreat back to my old self, not my best, and only me. It's a tide that I must flow with.

Often it shows me my worst self over and over—selfish, impatient, angry, scared, and blaming. And I feel as certain of all these things as I was of the Light and the possibilities of other things a short time before.

# Section 3

## The AIDS War Begins

What I Saw                          55

The Time of Long Goodbyes           57

AIDS in the Big House               59

Mikel's Phone Call                  60

Lubbock, Texas                      62

Dying Right on Time                 68

Last Visit with Bill                71

Nobody Cares                        74

Twenty Years in the AIDS War        76

World AIDS Day—Recollections        78

# What I Saw

*1994*

*What did I see in the first thirteen years of the AIDS epidemic?*

I saw a sixteen-year-old boy, sick as a dog—long before we even knew it was a virus—ask me, "Will I ever have sex again?"

I saw a sixty-year-old man thrown out of a hospital and limping back home to the school bus he lived in parked in the alley behind deserted houses.

I saw a baby live years and years and years after he was not supposed to—and still is.

I saw a man, one of the first diagnosed with AIDS in the U.S., spend fourteen years reaching for his own soul, more peaceful and happy the less body he had. And he still is.

I watched a dear friend get healthy for the first time in years because of new drug, and watched him die because the drug company stopped making it saying it cost too much.

I saw a drag queen jump on top of a police car in the middle of an AIDS demonstration at the National Institutes of Health, whip out a box of Dunkin Doughnuts, and yell, "Coffee Break!"

I saw a great singer go blind with one cough.

I saw a linguist, who went blind and lost his legs and his mind, keep saying, "Don't underestimate me!"

I saw a young Christian afraid to tell his church and family.

I saw a junkie jailed for gay bashing grow into an elder who saved others with his humor and honesty.

I saw young girls and boys trying to get free of drugs long enough to have a clean life before facing death.

I saw a parade of lovers helping each other get ready to go.

I saw a bank teller pick up my check with two pencils after he saw it was from an AIDS organization.

I saw a man so covered with cancer his own mother wouldn't touch him.

I saw a man's scrotum swell larger than a basketball while his mind dissolved.

I saw a Mexican village, where whole families—father, mother, and children, who sold their blood for money for food—were infected by the blood mobile that used the same needle on hundreds of people.

I saw AIDS workers weep with fatigue and young gay boys thrown out of their homes in the name of Christianity.

I saw governments spend billions on war and haggle about thousands of dollars for their own people.

I saw hookers become health educators and bar owners become activists.

I saw a Surgeon General say nothing about AIDS as the death toll surpassed the American dead from Viet Nam.

I saw a drug company make a pill that poisoned many people, sell it for 1000 times what it cost, and convince the public it was the best drug.

I saw cowards flee in terror, and I saw the courageous dig in.

I saw a gay blood drive by the Red Cross in 1976 with dyke nurses and faggot doctors, and that memory is already an antique.

I saw myself age and grow.

I saw a monastery where all the priests were gay and never said the G word.

I saw more dying people than both of my Viet Nam vet brothers saw. And I will see more soon.

I saw lovely people endure enormous pain and reveal the essence of life over and over and over.

The AIDS War Begins

# The Time of Long Goodbyes

*Written before effective AIDS drugs were available*

We are living now in the time of the long goodbyes. A moment when you or I or someone we love receives the word—the diagnosis of HIV infection—and begins to count time.

We begin to notice the years and their haste. We notice the moment and its merciless close-up on the now—the feelings of now, the perspective of now, the loss of seeing this moment pass and the loss of all tomorrows. Then our attention is diverted back to watching the procession of life.

We are living in the time when the news of 1985 becomes the support group of 1988 and the memorial service some time hence. This is the time when the numbers of the dead and the dying are the nightmares we dreamed only in sleep and never spoke of. And the one you couldn't bear to know would be next has been followed by so many others that you could not bear to know would be the next, and the next, and the next. And the horrible has become the usual.

We have struggled to find the beauty in the burning and the wisdom in the searing. We struggle to cry enough, for the losses outnumber each moment we give to grief. Who would ever think so much hurt could be seen over the years to inform us and create a culture of epidemic life and careers and a vocabulary and raging politics and bring out the best in so many and the worst in at least as many.

The word comes and life changes and gets sorted out to its most basic elements. What does it mean to be here? What needs to be done so the time here is made cleaner and clearer? And how much time do I have? Can I face such pure pain? How can I bear a broken heart? Can I move from just cleaning out old dirt to reaching for new ground? What will a slip near the cliff edge bring?

And the word does not mean leaving now. It's not the car accident that rips life away or the heart attack that leaves corpses blue. It's the word that the dying that we will all do is on its way, right now at some unknown speed but with our name, or the name of the one we love most, or the one we just met, or the one we think least strong.

It's all set now. The ride is happening. The roller coaster has left the entrance with your ticket stamped. And all your muscle and knowledge from a whole life gets pushed into deciding what you will scream, and that's your biggest choice—your chance to respond.

And the time will go slow too, and linger, and pause. And what it means to be here and see it all from too many sides will shift and show darkness and light as old friends. And be more beautiful than a heart can bear. And shine light more bright than can ever be hidden. And ask more than we have, and give too much and too much and too much.

# AIDS in the Big House

*February 1986*

The prison wall is the biggest thing in this little New York town near the Canadian border. We are checked for contraband and led through several gates to the chief guard. "Have you ever taught in a prison before?" I lie and say, "Of course."

From the audience of a hundred men, a tall handsome man raises his hand and asks if there is any suspicion that the AIDS epidemic is planned. "Do any rich white folks have it?" In a voice a bit black and very faggy I say, "Well, you know, Rock Hudson didn't live downtown." They all laugh very loud.

For the first time I am teaching in a maximum security prison about AIDS. Their laughter is good and rids me of the doubt I had about reaching them. They've wanted to know about AIDS since an inmate died last summer and another last week. In the last month, the local hospital has refused prisoners with AIDS, and all the new cases have overflowed the prison clinic into the locked psychiatric ward.

The last time someone with AIDS died here, the guards took the sheets out into a field and burned them. Such is the level of fear and ignorance five years into the epidemic. The warden has brought us in against the wishes of the superintendent. He knows that education is needed to help the staff and the inmates. He'll announce our visit after we've left.

The inmates are scared. The news I have to give them is hard. By sharing needles they have been at risk for a few years now. They may have already passed the virus on to a wife and perhaps a child-to-be.

I am as clear and tender as I can be. This is a painful witness.

# Mikel's Phone Call

*March 2004*

A long time ago, there was a man I gave seventy-five massages to in the year before he died. We would work once or twice a week at his apartment because he could no longer walk or drive. He paid me almost nothing because all his savings and possessions were being drained by an illness that we had only just gotten a name for. The flock of diseases he courted was doing the new things that would soon make this epidemic famous. There were not yet drugs for these new hurts, so the hurts got worse and worse. He had only been diagnosed a year and already his six-foot frame barely carried 120 pounds. He had fevers day and night, barely slept more than an hour at a time, couldn't take food, and hurt all over.

I was scared and very new to life in the epidemic. He became my teacher. I would set up my massage table, spread the sheets, and set out oil. Then I helped him to the table, slowly, slowly— each week, more slowly. All the while he filled me in on the news: What was the latest from the doctor? Did I hear that the AIDS project lost its funding but found a new director? The pain in his belly is worse from the medicines to help the infection in his lungs. He's sold his dining room set to pay rent. His ex will visit from California next week. The landlord almost found out he has AIDS.

As a young man, he was outed and dishonorably discharged from the Navy, and lost his wife and children in a nasty divorce. He then became a high-priced prostitute just long enough to set up trust funds for his children. Later he worked as a bartender and a waiter. In his spare time, he became head of a charity that raised thousands of dollars for children's hospitals by putting on drag balls, with himself in the most fabulous outfits of feathers, lace, and leather. His last appearance for this group was in a wheelchair still looking the tall handsome boyish man with a breathtaking smile.

In a year's time, I learned the contours of his body better than my own. He loved deep work at the shoulders and the lightest touch at his belly. He often went to sleep while I worked on him, partly because his pain left and he felt safe, partly because the fevers kept him exhausted and he slept at all odd times. His nightmares and daytime fears of dying filled his hours and stole much of his rest. Like most people, he didn't mind the idea of being dead so much as the idea of dying slowly and in pain. For a

The AIDS War Begins

year he told me he would get better and live a long time. I could feel the tension in his voice and throughout his body when he tried to push this as reality. I never said anything to disagree. I knew I saw something different but I wasn't there to argue. He was completely entitled to his own schedule and process.

One day as I worked very tenderly over the belly, I could feel his body calling me to linger there as my hands became warmer and warmer. His breathing was getting slower and deeper. Slowly I began to rock my body just a bit from my heels and soon something shifted deep inside him. Not an organ or muscle. Not breath or food. But something deeply held. Something heavy and old moved to another place and got lighter. Soon I felt a great sadness within me and looked down to see his closed eyes weeping. He made no effort to stop the tears. He had finally come to the place of grieving the passing of his own life. We never spoke of this.

Weeks later as we began another massage he mentioned that the phone might ring and it would be a call that he would have to take. When I had worked my way down the first leg, the call came. "Hello? Yes. Yes, I know honey. It'll be all right. Of course it's OK. Yes, I know. It's very hard. I love you too. Yes, goodbye."

As he lay back he said, "Sorry for the interruption. He's dying too. He called to say goodbye this afternoon because he's going to pull his oxygen off tonight while he's alone. He'll be gone by morning. He was a lovely man. Could you do some extra work on the back of my neck today? My body just melts when you go deep there."

# Lubbock, Texas

*April 1991*

I'm flying to Texas, my first time there, to do some AIDS work. I am partly excited and partly scared and partly wondering if I'll have enough energy to do all the work scheduled. I'm tired from the work I've been doing at home, which is mostly delving with a therapist into my hurt as a child. It's exhausting and it takes up much of the space in my thoughts and emotions.

I got a letter from Cecilia in August asking if I could do some teaching in Lubbock to people with AIDS and caregivers. And now, from April 4 to 6, I will give two lectures and two workshops, be interviewed by a newspaper journalist, spend half a day doing home visits to offer body work, and whatever else comes up. I feel well prepared. And I have moved from being reluctant to leave Marshall and our little house to being excited to be working in a totally new place with all new people.

It's my fourth day here now. I got in about 5 p.m., Wednesday night. Cecilia and Ed are wonderful hosts who have made me feel very welcome.

*Thursday*

Thursday morning Roy and his Aunt Linda took me to Carl's house. Roy is an AIDS educator with the South Plains AIDS Resource Center (SPARC). Linda is a massage therapist who'll begin work in the epidemic soon. Carl's mother has been taking care of him at home as he enters the final stages of AIDS. She is very old and very tired. She lost another son just months before.

Carl is a pioneer. He was one of the early AIDS workers in Lubbock. He helped many people feel less isolated, gave hugs to show others not to be afraid to touch the newly ill. He helped many people to die. All when he wasn't waiting tables. And now his weight is very low. He has difficulty walking. I have been warned that he is very angry and bitter, that I should be prepared to face someone who doesn't want help.

But today he's calm and welcoming. He talks quietly about the past, and now about where he's lived in Texas and the early days of the epidemic in Lubbock. He's lying on the couch in the living room. Carl's mom and Roy watch us from the dining room. Linda watches and listens from a chair nearby. She wants ideas on how to approach massage for people with AIDS.

The AIDS War Begins

First, I work on Carl's feet with oil, a slow massage, and energy work. He likes it very much and says in a soft voice that his feet haven't been touched this way in many years. His talking slows and gets softer. His Texas drawl makes each phrase feel like the prelude to sleep. I do some energy work in the air over him.

"I can really feel that in my organs like a breeze." His liver and spleen are enlarged and hurt as they rub against his ribs. As I touch him in various places to reduce his pain, he closes his eyes and gets close to sleep. I work half an hour. Before he finishes talking, he mentions that he is closer to emotional acceptance of being in final stages now. The fight in him is less.

In the afternoon, Jerry, another SPARC staffer, takes me to a newspaper office to be interviewed by the religion editor. Beth asks good questions and I find myself trying to answer in quotable sound bites which seem to be phrases from my letters and teaching. She copies verbatim. I mention ritual abuse in my clients. She wants to know more. She's trying to sort through the hysteria of the fundamentalists to whatever evidence there is that a newspaper reporter can cover. She says the stories are too outlandish and numerous to be true.

"That's what they use to say about rape," I tell her.

She says, "That's what's still said about rape in Texas."

*Thursday Night*

Thursday night I speak at the hospital about healing from trauma. Some of the boys with AIDS in the audience have tears in their eyes and are nodding as I go on about the effects of hard times. About twenty-five people have come. Two of the people with AIDS have their fathers with them. It strikes me as particularly Texan or Southern that there are fathers and other relatives stretching to learn whatever will be of help. It also makes me feel like an orphan knowing that such a choice would never be offered to me.

I talk for an hour. It makes me self-conscious to be filmed, but I enjoy the task of teaching and there seems to be great appetite for the ideas. The questions are few but good. The applause and joy make clear the feeling that it's been appreciated. Always there is a rush of need following these tasks. A young woman works with a neonatal unit and wants me to do training with nurses. Also, there's a child who is unresponsive but no one can figure out what's wrong—can I visit him? A therapist wants work on her back and arms right then and there. She is locked up in pain between scapulae. There's a sort of shadow there I cannot budge, but I give some ideas for work.

A young man is introduced to me. He's been very teary through my talk. He is newly sober and now tested positive for HIV. He needs lots of encouragement to keep paying attention to his life and stay out of the numbness of using drink on the pain and depression. It distracts me a great deal that he is extremely attractive, but I speak to him as the sainted teacher healer he seeks.

*Friday Morning*

Friday morning I present a massage workshop at the hospital. There are five men with HIV, Linda, and some SPARC staff—one a woman doing education to women in prostitution and jails. A hospital physical therapist comes by and I work on her. We discuss bodywork in Lubbock. It's meager. I work on the director of SPARC. He's a large man who has done much good. He has kept many ways of his salesman/business days and carries a giant mobile phone the size of a shoe. He is always cheery and tense. Perhaps he will discern the differences between community health care and business soon.

I work on a tall young man who is newly sober. He takes the energy work in deeply. His family smothered his ego in his teenage years. He's been kept very young with no personal power because of this.

In two hours I present an easy massage form and beginning energy work to nine people, most work on each other. I work on a few in obvious need.

*Friday Afternoon*

That afternoon, I work on seven men at the SPARC office. They have all heard testimony from Carl that I am worth seeing. Most are in okay health. Some are in trouble. All have amazing stories of how HIV changed their lives and how they are coping. I try to gather an essence from each one as to history and current situation. With this I can use my empathy and get clues about where to work. It also creates a bond I rely on for them to let me in.

One fellow lost a marriage and his business with his diagnosis. He is misshapen now as his kidneys and liver malfunction. His kids have been teased at school about having an AIDS daddy. Another man, a grandfather, is somewhat ill himself. He lost a long-term lover to AIDS, and now has a young lover with AIDS. The young lover loses his breath to asthma each evening. He thought he had outgrown it but it's returned now with AIDS. They are all mainly strong, kind, and in good spirits, though fear and some pain lurks. I am with each one alone for half an hour. They lie on the short couch, and I move my hands through the air above them, then touch their bodies. Every one relaxes and calms down. One sleeps.

Before sunset I am taken to a nursing home to work on a young Chicano man. He came down with severe PCP pneumonia in February and went from award winning gymnast to death's door in three days. He did this at a friend's house because of a drunken step-daddy's abuse of mom. This young man was also sexually abused by his grandfather, who died of a mysterious disease years ago. He is bright eyed and adorable. He's very excited about leaving the nursing home for a weekend at home with mom. As I work my hands over him, he watches and smiles. I ask him if he can feel the effects as my hands pass over him. "Oh yes. My mother has done the same work to help me. But she holds an egg in one hand. Then you are supposed to crack the egg into a glass and by its color tell what illness you have." I ask him what has been the cause of his remarkable recovery. "A good family," he says.

Later I talk with a woman who brought this young man to the hospital. He'd been a boyfriend to her daughter. After his diagnosis the daughter tested negative for HIV. Now that they've broken up and the girl is out of state, her mother still keeps track of the boy. Her brother is also positive and so weaves the web of caring for those around us, hoping our loved ones away are being taken care of.

*Friday Night*

Tonight there's a potluck supper with Quakers and others. We talk over ideas and journeys. I avoid a chance to hold forth. I am very tired from my work. When I go to bed at 10 p.m., I am dragging and really missing Marshall. I have one full day to go.

Saturday I teach a massage workshop at the MCC church. Three men with HIV have come with their fathers. I demonstrate a simple massage on a mother and then we get into pairs. I work on a man who had a paralyzing stroke on his right side three weeks earlier. His mother and father are with him and listen intently to all I have to share. The father whispers to me in the slowest of heavy Texas accent, "It's HIV." I work on his head and neck and both arms and legs with energy. He rests deeply and moves a little better after lying there a while.

I can feel his parents' hope upon my shoulders that I would be a "real" healer and make him walk again. When he moves his arm in a new way that he couldn't before, they are grateful and swear to practice daily what I have shown. Meanwhile the church is full of pairs moving each other into stages of massage mellowness. The whole room softens.

Mikki, whom I met the day before and who has been video taping all my teaching, comes up to me and whispers that Brenda needs work from me. She has tricked Brenda into coming by requesting her help with the video camera. Two years ago Brenda pulled several people out of a fire in a nursing home. She saved several lives and inhaled chemical fumes destroying 85% of her lungs. When it comes time to teach energy work, I ask Brenda if I can work on her. She comes up reluctantly and lies down.

I do some teaching as I begin to work on her. Her breath is quick and shallow like a kitten or a rabbit. She lies there without any relaxing for a long time. As I move my hands through the air above her I can feel the sense of sticky damage and flimsy tissue in her lungs.

It isn't until I am nearly finished demonstrating the energy work form on Brenda that I begin to discuss how everyone in the room could focus their care on this one person and amplify my work. I also talk about the difficulty of receiving. I speak slowly and softly. As I approach her heart I say, "Yes, when the shit hits the fan, it's really time to lie down and let someone love you. It's good to let someone love you. It's not easy but it's very good."

Just then I feel a barrier lift and a huge sadness move through me, bringing me to tears. I silently work on her head and finish up by asking the twenty observers to team up. I work some more on Brenda and she goes into a deep sleep for the next hour and a half. After that she has lots of energy. Later she goes to an amusement

The AIDS War Begins

park with friends. I watch each pair of workers and see much lovely work going on.

I kneel by the mother working on her paralyzed son. "Now, Mama," I say, "You are doing beautiful work and you're remembering to use your love and not your worry, aren't you?"

She looks at her son with great love and says, "Oh yes."

I say, "I know it's not easy, but it's best."

She says, "You're right."

# Dying Right on Time

*March 2004*

I drive to a big city to attend Meeting for Worship where I know someone who is dying. As he enters and makes his way across the floor, I can feel the whole Meeting gazing on his obviously painful, frail, and disappearing body with a mixture of love and horror. It's as though a war has come home with wounded and fighting all over, everywhere screaming, "This is what AIDS looks like! This is what old age looks like on someone in his 30's!!" Few speak in that Meeting for Worship, but the sound of his labored breath and cough are like fog horns in the distance warning of danger.

After Meeting, the dying one lies on a bench in a back row. He hurts too much to sit up. His lover is near and so are several members of his care committee. He is under a blanket. By and by I sit near him and carefully make contact.

There are obstacles.

First, I have a bit of a reputation for showing up when things are getting very bad. And there is very particular etiquette around who mentions dying first especially if the dying one hasn't said anything. Also he and I are not old friends. We have known each other a long time, but there is an obstacle to our loving, which I suspect is that we have similar early hurt that resonates too loudly when we are together. I had mentioned this to him in a note a month before but promised to come help him if he wanted.

In truth I am here because his best friend is a dear old friend of mine who is his neighbor and also has AIDS. I am really here to help my dear friend as someone he loves prepares to die.

I reach over the back of the bench where he lies and begin to talk and touch. He is grateful for any help with the enormous pain he has been in for over a month now. The cancer is throughout his body. He is so thin and bony, each touch must be made with absolute grace so as not to be invasive. I can lift some of the pain, but it is set so deeply in the physical body that I cannot help much, only relieve the tension gathered and accumulated around the pain.

He is glad for what I can do in the twenty minutes we work. He feels a little better and asks to be taken home. We make a date to work the next night.

I speak with members of his care committee who are stunned at this rapid decline and frustrated by his reluctance to receive care. Independence and fear of intimacy clog the corridor to his heart. I offer a few ideas. I caution that he could very well die ahead of everyone's expected schedule for him. This committee is in good shape, and he is well cared for.

The next night I work on him for an hour. His apartment looks like a dorm room at end of semester, half packed and almost ready to go, messy. He takes the energy work in eagerly. I start with his feet for more grounding and to help move his awareness out of his head. There is a problem with being too smart and thinking too much which can cause us to miss the messages from the body and the meaning of an illness. And he is extremely smart and very—too much—in his head.

He asks why I am not at his chest and belly where all the hurt is. I tell him it's because he's so smart and thinking too much. He grins at this. As I move up to his head I can feel a deep and thorough spiritual life has come about in this time of decline. He is telling everyone that he is going to pull through this sick period and get well again. His friends want to believe him and hope he's right, but he has sunk so low.

I can feel the difference between what he says out of his intellectual hope of getting well and his deeper spiritual knowing that time is short and he will die soon. He is ready to die. He is weary from the pain and exhausted by the care of so many who have moved into his private and very independent life.

There is no tension or denial in his reluctance to speak of his own dying. On the one hand he gives the message that he wants to live, a message he thinks will help others and be positive. On the other hand, he has no more fight in him. His very full life is now obstructed beyond what he can change.

And his spiritual life has come to a fullness, using his illness to encourage patience in others. Denial is more hollow. Denial says there is not a problem and this not only sounds hollow but has a background of fear that can be heard by listening with a very soft focus. He has none of this, no fear. I am certain it has to do with his use of prayer while sick and that he is surrounded by much love. Spiritually he has come to peace. He rests deeply, and I let myself out to visit with my good friend next door.

~

This dear one is healthy, perhaps more so than many other times in his life. He is happy and has made a life that combines hard work, a ministry of serving others by teaching non-violence in schools around the world, and love as good as any that can be found anywhere. But this dying next door is a very big challenge. I fear for his grief. I listen and say what I have felt and offer what little wisdom I have for such an impossible situation.

I have loved this old friend for nearly twenty years. We know each other's dirty laundry, the rough and the smooth, the wisdom and ignorance of having come into our fifties. He is trying to weave the balance of helping a close friend to die of the same disease that he has, to give some of what is needed without losing heart and hope for his own life. Such is the nature of spiritual life for gay men at the turn of this century.

His is a problem of the category called "too-much." It's too much for those of us who are teachers and writers and others accustomed to explaining the nature of things as a way of coping and enduring with them. This too-much cannot be accomplished with logic or intellect. We must give ourselves the freedom and the time and space to scream and run, shit, or go blind with all the feelings that we cannot name or sort. This calls for a kind of faith in the divine madness for anyone who seeks to understand the hell-end of a life of numerous nasty diseases. It's the use of extremes for balance. And it is the historically common ground of troublemakers, spiritual and/or political, who, if lucky, become cultural heroes when they are dead and no longer around to bother their tribe directly. Gandhi, ML King, or Mother Jones would not be easy neighbors to have, but can be admired for being true and faithful to important causes.

A few days later at home in Vermont I get a call that the dying one, to everyone's surprise, died suddenly. It was a blessed and peaceful dying surrounded by love. He was helped right to the door. The convener of his care committee was truly chosen to be there, to be of use even though the task raises new and old pain around the understanding of giving. She was blessed to be the one to guide him to the door. And it is a real grace that she can see all this without ignoring or denying or getting lost in her pain of a dear friend's death. This is the real nature of ministry.

The AIDS War Begins

# Last Visit with Bill

*June 4, 2000*

Bill is sitting on the couch watching some old funny movie. A T-shirt hangs from bony shoulders and lands down by his diaper. He's been wearing diapers for three months now. His arms and legs are so thin I can't help but stare. How could this stallion of a man, this mile runner, this gym bunny and late night disco sweat dancer be reduced so quickly?

He moves his eyes to see who just came into the room. But his head and eyes move slowly, so slowly you wonder if his mind is still the sharp clear library of spiritual life and nonviolent conflict resolution. Can he follow the conversation now? Can he join at the normal speed? Do we all talk too fast for him now?

The others leave for a bit, and we're alone. I sit next to him and put my arm over his shoulder with a hand resting where I can feel the heat of his skin, the bones pushing through his too thin flesh, and his relief at being touched and held.

"You saw your folks?" I ask.

"Yes. I gave my mother a hug and began to cry and say, 'I don't want to die.' She was very good. We hugged and cried. It's very important to do that with a mother."

With just that much I knew he had done years of bridge-building in a few moments. Even the effort to tell me that much and recall the impact leaves him short of breath.

"Let's go out on the deck," he says.

I help him rise with all my balance, using careful handholding and some strength to steady him. With his hands on my shoulders, we shuffle down the hall like kids playing trains.

He sits down on the chaise like he's setting down a load of bricks. Pillows are brought to fit him just right. He looks out into the trees, has a blanket put round his legs with big slippers sticking out.

I can't take my eyes off him. It's part my love and part disbelief and part knowing there is so little time. I watch him drift off in little naps. I watch him fumble with a cigarette and lighter. I see him barely able to lift a glass of water. Its weight from table to lips asks too much of his arm and hand.

On the couch and on the chaise he tries to listen to what's being said. He's listening on the edge here and there, and only engaged if it's funny enough. This makes me want to say anything that will make him laugh. And when I accomplish this, I feel as though I have given a familiar gift from our twenty years as close friends.

At times the stimulus of people or the wind or some change within his body causes him to fold in on himself, and I wonder where he is and if there is any comfort there. What is he thinking about? What is he feeling in his body? Can I be of comfort, or would it be interrupting? And when did I become such a mother? I would do anything to help.

I give him massage and energy work as much as he will allow. The back muscles are eager for the warm touch, the small muscles pulled so tight between each bone. His long legs loosen as I work down from the narrow hips. The sore at the bottom of his spine has a virus that eats through skin and must be kept covered with ointment and dressing. His head begs for more touch as though each massage stroke of the forehead, the scalp, the cheeks, the neck is a kiss he's been waiting for, a kiss of calm moving throughout him. He lets go of all the too-much and sleeps for a little while. And when he awakes he is refreshed, more talkative, and more funny. There is so much virus raging in him now that he steals life energy from whoever is close. I would gladly pour into him for weeks and months to have him be here longer.

"I've been planning my memorial service. There'll be no sloppy or undisciplined ministry." He wants a speaker, a few songs, and time for people to say what they remember about him. There are so many memories I can't share with anyone because he told me not to tell anyone ever. That's the kind of friends we were—old war stories of sexual adventures and romantic stories of the one that got away or the one we got rid of.

We had seen each other fall in love with men we found by accident. We had seen the love slowly become larger over the years and change us from the inside. We were happy for each other. We liked seeing who we were each becoming.

He was the kind of teacher you would wish for every child or adult. He shared a love of life, a twinkle in the eye, a light step of joy, and a delight in seeking with thousands of people over the years—thousands. He taught children and teachers how to use non-violence in schools. He was known in Moscow and Belfast. His books sold well in Australia and Europe.

What will it be like for him to separate from his body? Will he remember a similar feeling from another time—the fall into love,

The AIDS War Begins

the lift of smoke from the pipe, the handsome stranger who thought he was to be adored? And who will meet him on the other side? Will it be Fred, or Lydia, or the grandmother he made doughnuts with every Saturday?

When it comes time to say goodbye, I try not to cry. My arm around his back, my head touching his, I whisper, "I love you so much. I'll be back next week. And I'll be thinking of you the whole time I'm not here."

I get teary and my voice thickens, but he can't see my eyes red and wet. I am hoping not to upset him. But as he hugs others, I stand back and watch, and I know this really is goodbye. As others move towards the door, he says, "I haven't given up."

I lean my head to his and say, "Wear it as long as thou canst.* I just want you to stick around as long as it's fun."

"Yes," he says, "as long as it's fun."

Such a Light as this we shall not see again for a long time. God help us all to carry on life without his smile right here guiding us.

# Nobody Cares

*March 2004*

It's mid-morning, and not everyone is really awake, but we have gathered for the grieving circle. The group is stuck in not knowing one another, yet over-burdened with all the too-much of living with AIDS. There is a deep division between black and white and women and men. We settle into some quiet. After a time, I set an empty chair next to me. It's there for anyone in the circle who wants to name his or her losses. After each one finishes speaking, I ask, "May we hold you?" They need only to nod to receive the comfort of touch after sharing their truth.

The first to come forward is a very dramatic theater professional. Draped in silk and the kind of pissy attitude one must truly work to achieve, he lost his best friend the night before. He is clearly in pain, but his expensive new clothes and excessive angst draws little compassion from the circle. He is afraid for himself, and that fear looks self-indulgent to this circle of streetwise veterans. A few more people come forward to name their losses. The momentum of people caring for one another's wounds slowly begins to fill our sails. But still there is mostly holding back.

Finally, the oldest woman shuffles up. She takes in the group with a look that surrenders all defense without losing any power. "I got no one who cares I'm dying. Not family or friends. I am lost as far as I can be and no home to find. Ain't nobody cares this black junkie hooker is an old woman scared of dying. I used to be somebody's mother, sister, child, and now I am only alone. I ain't got nobody cares I'm dying."

She is a little teary, but mostly she is filled with radiant energy that comes from speaking so fiercely of her life. We are all stunned at the honesty this woman had shared with a circle of strangers. For the first time, all the women come forward, lay hands on her head and shoulders, arms around her back and waist, rock her gently, and take away the only thing possible which is this moment of loneliness.

The last to take the chair is a young man who cries as he tells us that he is sad about dying, but what really hurts is all of us being so separated from each other. In a few words he grieves the loss of humanity and compassion throughout the country—across gender, orientation, and color lines. He is so generous in his care for the whole beyond himself that his weeping draws in the whole group.

We rock ourselves around him, finally gathered together as one.

# 20 Years in the AIDS War

*March 2004*

Two people called for help today. I spent a long time on the phone reminding them of what they knew about their own healing and encouraging them to hold on until the pain passed, the pain always passes. Sometimes I could help shape the question that could bring their focus to where Light needed shining. And I made them laugh.

Yesterday was the anniversary of Bill Kreidler's death. Many were the times when I called Bill and he reminded me that the pain always passed—pain, depression, fear. And he made me laugh, bless him, he could make me laugh more than anyone. Like all good teachers he was good at reminding one of the long view, especially when panic brought into focus only the now. He told me stories of himself that made his foolishness seem like a bright gleaming joke just waiting for some down-in-the-dumps friend to hear. I remember his living now more than his dying, one of the mercies that comes after a year passing. But I've missed him very much the last month or two. I had hoped we would be old Quaker queens together, reminding each other to take our teeth out and put in our pills and not confuse the two.

The time came later when I would no longer ask of him but would only give and provide as best I could. His humor was worn down as his body became less and less. He had no capacity for pain and was not easy at first with needing help from others. That move from private independent living to publicly known illness and dependency was gently done with much help from his partner each day. Only once in the very early stages did he roll in my arms weeping in great despair. Oh, to have that burden of deep loving again with him. But it was not to be.

When AIDS came into our lives, Bill knew friends with it first. I got into it later via strangers I came to love in their dying. But Bill was helping friends with it from the beginning.

It's hard to believe that twenty years has already come and gone in the AIDS wars. So much has happened and there is still so much to do. Last week, I called Jason, an old friend diagnosed in 1981. He was in the first PWA support group with Michael Callen in NYC. He's been very ill several times, but is well and very much alive after all these years. He lectures in teaching hospitals to young doctors now, so much more the expert than the professionals. His Buddhist leanings have helped him to watch for the underlying meanings with each new illness and in choosing which medicines to take or continue with. As with so many of us, he is a reluctant student, given to overstayed bouts at the party instead of prostrating at the monastery. And then choosing the monastery realizing it was the first best choice.

I am also missing Claude Branque of Seattle—infamous gay Quaker healer faerie. AIDS took him in the early nineties after a dozen years of illness. Claude was one of those shining examples of the merely appearing eccentric actualizing as a guide into the mysteries of spiritual life—the untidy corners of spiritual life where more than a single theology reins and reveals its selves. He once reached over the phone lines across the continent to move a lymphatic lump in my breast, melting it to nothing. He could feel when I was working too hard from 3,000 miles away and would call to interrupt the intensity. He once found a very large stone in the woods he wanted for his garden. He spoke with the stone, asking for permission of the stone to move it and requesting its help to lift a weight well beyond his capacity. The stone agreed and came home with him. I saw that stone in his garden after his death and am quite sure no common man could have moved it. Claude helped me to feel more common and less afraid even as I learned the inner workings of pain and suffering.

With this twenty-year marker, I am trying to rededicate myself to another twenty years in this work. There is so much good that needs doing. So many people who need the reminders that the pain will pass and the encouragement to hold on, and the stories of our foolishness to laugh at. God help us all to keep going. It might be that life is hard by its nature and made beautiful by our good and tender care of it.

# World AIDS Day—Recollections

*December 2009*

All day I've felt a bit sad. I've been remembering the arc of AIDS in my life, what I usually think of as the AIDS Wars. I remember hearing a little something in August of 1983, an article in *Time* magazine perhaps, about gay men getting cancer in San Francisco and New York. I was teaching in a summer camp and quite isolated.

But when I returned to massage school in Boulder, I began to learn more and seek out more information. I remember in October going to an informational meeting by the Colorado Department of Health and learning what little information they had. Maybe it was a virus. AIDS had not come forward as a specific disease and was not called AIDS yet. No one was sure how it was spread but probably by body fluids. Not sure about kissing, except gay men kiss their grandmothers, and grannies did not seem to have AIDS, the doctor said.

I called that doctor soon and offered to give massage to anyone in Colorado with AIDS, whether or not they could pay. Fortunately, the numbers were still in the single digits, and I did massage on four people very soon. Three became long-term clients. Two were dead in a few years. Many more were diagnosed and died quickly as we had so little understanding of the new diseases and none of the existing medicines worked.

Back in Vermont in 1985 I began teaching AIDS 101 at Quaker Meetings and in New York prisons. I became part of the Vermont People With AIDS Coalition and did tons of massage and teaching there. In 1986 my best friend got swollen lymph nodes, and though he wouldn't die for several years, my heart began to break.

I met Marshall and moved to Los Angeles, began to teach with AIDS, Medicine & Miracles (AM&M) and did massage with Michael Callen of the Flirtations over the years. And then we moved to Washington, D.C., where John Meyer got me hooked up with AIDS services, and I was hands-on in several hospitals, teaching buddy teams, and just beginning work with tortured refugees for a change of pace. It was good to work with people who were not dying.

About this time, my best friend began to be seriously ill. And that long vigil of support and saying goodbye began. More friends became ill. Any illness I felt was terrifying. I was now deeply in love and married in all senses but the legal one and feared greatly that one of us would become ill, and we'd be among the many sinking low and disappearing and then part of the great flood of memorials. I was doing grieving circles at night at Friends General Conference Gathering because there was a need from more grieving than usual life allowed, and these circles were crowded with amazing stories and so many people.

When we moved back to Vermont in 1990, I was relieved of doing regular hospital visits and the density of memorials, but became part of the rural work of education and service. Bill, my best friend, began to decline slowly. He would have a rally and stay strong for a bit. And then some other infection would bring him low again. And his true love did an amazing job of care, beyond what I could do, I am sure. By the time Bill died I was nearly numb to the great pain of the world in this pandemic. It was my coming of age in my early thirties and now squashed my heart and hope almost two decades later.

I still teach about AIDS when I'm invited. And I still lay hands on people with AIDS as a massage therapist and energy worker. A couple of friends, still living, are among the very first people diagnosed in NYC in the very early 80's.

Recently I worked with a young doctor from Rwanda whose life work has become pediatric AIDS in a children's hospital. He told me he felt numb and had no emotions left. We discussed avoiding burnout, the advanced form. And we did some hands-on work that felt full of Light and well guided from on high. He told me that in Rwanda he had not seen the worst. I was afraid to ask what that meant in Rwandan terms.

And this summer I'll return to an AIDS conference where I've been teaching for more than twenty years. I'll see old dear ones and laugh and clap my hands as I walk to them calling out in a loud voice, "Oh For God's Sake, Are You Still Alive?!" And we'll hug and laugh to still be here, still be doing the work, still be grateful for so many things. And I'll talk quietly with the newly diagnosed, young girls and boys and some grandmothers, and find some ways to help them relax and maybe to laugh and maybe dare to hope that as bad as the news is, they can still do life and do it in a big way with this new family as an anchor.

I am so honored and exhausted and proud of what we've survived. I can't imagine a life without this education that I never signed up for. I'm so happy to have learned how to get up each day and work in hell. And that to go in smiling created the best chance to carry Light as far into those dank corners as possible. I still miss Bill, especially on this day, and listen to his speeches on tape and get teary. But I remember his living more than his dying and his laughter more than his tears. I was so dearly looking forward to getting old with him. Now I just remember how it felt to be with him and when I see some handsome man walking down the beach, some part of me smiling inside says—hey Bill, look at that!

It's life itself that draws us on, that bright Light and hope that we'll see how lovely life is.

The AIDS War Begins

# Section 4

# Hands On

Do Quakers Heal?                               83

Earlham School of Religion                     87

Flowing Waters from the Source                90

Five Years in Solitary                         94

What Is It and
Where Does It Come From?                       96

Still Learning                                 99

Surrender Over and Over                       101

Abandoned                                      102

Queries for Caregivers                        104

Healing Notes                                  106

# Do Quakers Heal?

*February 2001*

On a snowy winter weekend in February 2001, twenty Friends gathered at Powell House, a gracious old mansion, turned Quaker conference center in Old Chatham, New York. The focus of the gathering was to share our knowledge of healing work as Quakers.

The idea for gathering Northeastern Friends on healing came from a previous workshop called "Healing as Quaker Faith and Practice." There was a desire among some Friends of Baltimore and New York Yearly Meetings to have a network to share information and support for those doing healing work. Most Friends were from New York, with others from Maryland, Pennsylvania, and New England. Frank Massey of Sandy Springs, Maryland, did a wonderful job of setting tone and bringing us together with introductions and a planning session.

Setting our agenda on Friday evening included methods and training, stories of self-discovery, self-care, Meeting for Healing, and how each of us understood or described our gift. We seemed to have two common traits among us: we were all Quakers, although not all the same kind of Quaker, and we all had done some healing work that was Spirit-led. We were a wide range of ages and experience in this work.

## Forms of Healing Work

We had Meeting for Healing on Saturday and Sunday. There was some discussion of which forms we would use. The greatest desire seemed to be for hands-on work for those present. There was also a call to bring loved ones at home into the circle by calling their names, which we did on Saturday. Both Meetings had a clear sense of being grounded in the presence of the Spirit. Both Meetings brought deep changes of awareness and well-being, along with tears, to more than one person.

Meeting in a large group, we explored many topics. We had some wonderful sharing about Quaker history in healing work. Rosalind Zuses of Baltimore Yearly Meeting brought us details of the struggle to do healing work, stay in the Light and out of one's ego, and avoid persecution—a difficult balance for early Friends in England.

One session devoted to self-care brought Susan McLaren forward to share ideas from her two decades of work as a spiritual healer.

In small groups we shared our personal stories of being called to do healing work. Some of us have had training in the healing arts either by massage, energy work, or more traditional methods—more than one nurse was with us. Many of us came to this work by a leading and have our greatest confirmations by remaining faithful to this leading. Some of us describe our work solely as prayer, focusing healing energy without touch. Some of us use laying-on-of-hands without any movement such as massage strokes. Some work with both forms. Among the healers using touch, many methods of training have been used from Reiki, Therapeutic Touch, Healing Touch, and Swedish massage.

## What to Call Quakers Who Do Healing Work

The longest discussion was about the consequences of calling oneself a Quaker healer. There was concern that to do healing as Quakers do other ministries and not to name it was to hide one's Light under a bushel. Others feared that the title of Quaker healer would cause a public assumption of the healer working miracles on the sick. Others pointed to the history of early Friends doing healing work and "being in the power of the Lord." Some wanted to go part way with the naming by saying they were Friends with a healing ministry. Others wanted to be known as Quaker healers so as to be more forthright and advance this work within the Religious Society of Friends.

The talk moved from personal discomfort to what title would be most effective. In a changing culture where one wants to be grounded in Friends' tradition and not be confused with trendy New Age language or put people off with religiosity, how does one express a gift, a compassionate heart, and be of help to those in need of healing? What responsibility is taken when one offers help, and how does that change of name help? This includes the question of whose power is being named. Friends doing healing work in the name of Jesus wanted that to be clear in their naming. Some Friends wanted to claim the power of their participation while being very clear to name the source in all healing as divine. This discussion was inconclusive and will go on for some time.

## Earlier Gatherings

A few years before, a larger gathering of Quaker healers from across the U.S. was held at Pendle Hill, a Quaker study center in Wallingford, Pennsylvania. There was a similar feeling of dedication to being faithful to a leading and a very moving Meeting for Healing. The most obvious commonality was a passionate delight in finding a path that contributed to the common good while binding one closer to the Divine in direct experience. I believe such gatherings will increase. A sampling of workshops at Friends General Conference summer gathering over the past dozen years shows an evident and increasing interest among Friends to know more and do more work in this field. It was clear that Powell House will continue with this topic in various forms.

## Quaker History of Healing

Reconstituted by Henry Cadbury in 1948 and released by Quaker Press of FGC in 2000, *George Fox's 'Book of Miracles'* gives us a sense of the history of early Quakers in healing work. Then, as now, there were struggles with language, ego, and the consequences of naming a work or claiming certain spiritual gifts. Much of this work went underground and was missing or hidden during the 18th and 19th centuries. Intimate work and spiritual gifts always call for long slow careful learning. Such work is bound to face the obstacles of misunderstanding, misrepresentation, and fear or envy. History concurs.

## Quaker Healing Around the World

I began to survey Quakers worldwide about practices of Meeting for Healing in January 2000. Thirty questions have made their way to Friends around the globe. Friends in England and Australia have well-founded groups on healing. I've heard from Friends in several countries and will continue to collect material, hoping to do more writing as information comes in. It's clear that some Friends have long established traditions of Meeting for Healing, while others are just beginning to grow.

## A New Period in Quaker History?

Four periods of Quakerism were identified by Howard Brinton in *Friends for 300 Years*. In a paper for Oberlin College's Religion,

Health, & Spirituality class, Noah Hoskins-Forsythe suggests we may have entered a fifth period—The Convergence of Mysticism and Modern Medicine—because so many Friends are involved in healing work. Perhaps as more Friends devote faith and practice to healing, including the bridges between healing and peacemaking, we are headed for a new period in Quakerism. If so, the Light given through healing work in this period will require our careful use to share learning and responsibility. And, as always, staying in the Light will be the main challenge. Is it true that we are coming into a new time of Quaker healing? What are the people doing this work to be called? What language will reflect the clarity their actions enjoy now?

# Earlham School of Religion

*February 2004*

*How would you describe your spiritual work?*

I think using words to describe spiritual experience dilutes the reality because language is always insufficient but, given that caveat, here's what I know.

I have a gift for releasing pain. This gift comes upon me like a message in Meeting for Worship. I have to be listening at that higher level. It is not always available to me. I don't have control over when this gift is available, with whom it gets to be used or how. This gift is under my care, and mainly, I have to be faithful. In some ways, it has become as familiar as centering for worship. In some ways, it feels as though this gift is run by some committee upstairs.

I can set up time and people to work with, such as setting a time for a Meeting for Healing. But this means keeping spiritual disciplines so as to be ready when the hour comes. Whatever help I can be to one person I may not be to another, even in that same Meeting. The gift that comes through me is not of my choosing.

There is also a spontaneous aspect to my work. Someone asks for help, or I see someone needing help, or I walk into a room where I am to teach and a few people stand out. One listens both outwardly to what one can know and inwardly for "what Spirit wants" or guidance. I feel accompanied in my work by angels or spirit guides. I listen. Then with what I hear, I am able to go to work. At times I have a sudden flash of insight into the nature of someone's pain and how it can be moved. Other times, I can see clearly the nature of the pain and that I won't be able to move it— or more accurately, that it will not be given to me to move it. Whether such a determination is heavenly or cosmic timing, etiquette, the maturity of my ministry, or a bad hair day is beyond me. I do have a sense of trying to learn from all that is shown. I try not to push the holy river when I personally want something to be otherwise. I know that all that goes on has purpose, that nothing is random.

In my work, I have had visitations from Jesus, Mary, and the Buddha. Each of them guided my work. I did not call them; my sense is that they appeared in response to the prayers of the people I was helping. I can confirm that the good press we hear about these three is not even the beginning of the Light they have to offer.

I have some sense that worldly competence, such as being a massage therapist, serves me in knowing how the body is constructed. It is wonderful to be grounded in knowledge and skills. But for me, the more necessary parts of the work are reverence and faithfulness. A great deal of surrender is required. By that I mean I have to give up worldly ideas that limit my understanding of what's possible. It is the difference between hearing yourself and hearing Divine guidance. The practice of surrender is especially important when fear and anger are present.

*What's the place of your ministry in the context of the Society of Friends?*

I am less sure of this. I know some Friends sense, see, and know what my gift is and understand the care that I give to it. These Friends tend to support the effort. Other Friends are turned off by my calling myself a Quaker healer and can't be bothered to check further. There is a regard for eccentricity within the Society and a tradition of watching for what is felt to have deep spiritual roots, what "feels right." In these assessments by others, I have done quite well. It led to my being a Released Friend from my Monthly Meeting for fifteen years, a release I did not request but was offered—further confirmation that one's gift is told to one by his or her spiritual community, and that it is not self-generated.

There are signs that I have been doing this work long enough to have made some impact—keynotes and plenaries for several national conferences and Yearly Meetings, full workshops, good mention by others in their writings. On the other hand, I feel as though I have to be careful to live at the edge of the village with a lot of solitude. While I have acted in consultation with numerous clerks and committees, I am not on boards or committees myself.

*Are you in contact with the Friends Fellowship of Healing?*

The British Fellowship of Healing did reprint some of my writing, and we've had some correspondence. I have visited and would love to teach there in the future. The Fellowship in Australia has also reprinted some of my writings.

*What's the relationship between prayer and technique in your work?*

Prayer is the constant connection to following the process. For me the task of prayer is not necessarily the orthodox understanding of using particular words but rather a tone, almost a constant hum, which is my task to keep unbroken before, during, and after the work. Work without prayer would be like hammering nails with carrots—why bother? It's the quality of reverence, the depth of centering, that makes the experience productive, understandable, and life-changing. I have shown up to work tired, hung over, or grouchy, but handed myself over to be used, and the most beautiful grace has descended. I have learned that to show up with all my imperfections is better than not to show up at all. Imperfections need not be a source of guilt unless one is not working to lessen them.

*Do you have any ideas about why the Society of Friends suppressed their healing ministry in the 18th and 19th centuries?*

Cadbury's book says Friends caught hell from the government for doing healing work and then telling everybody about it. He also says that Friend George Fox was thought to be doing a bit too much personal public relations and thinking himself a bit too "chosen" for the comfort of other Friends. Not many Friends know of Fox's keeping a scorecard of God smiting Fox's enemies. These certainly contributed.

There was, and is now, also a desire to experience spiritual life as dispassionately, intellectually, and safely as possible. This would surely rule out touch and large involvement with issues of pain. In part this may be due to Quakerism being British. We might have seen a different history had Quakerism begun in, say, Italy. Much of the passion of spiritual life is done in the closet, in part because it is hard to manage aspects of faith for which we don't even have words. We don't burn witches now. We do other things to discourage spiritual life. But we are still greatly bothered, rather than intrigued, by what we cannot name or understand or see clearly or control. Historically, groups have cycles of dipping into great sources of power, experiencing corruption or misuse that can cause a withdrawal from that power, and then rediscovering that source later.

# Flowing Waters from the Source

*Talk at Friends World Committee on Consultation, 2003*

Friends, I am honored to speak with you tonight. I love to look at this group and see so many people who have done such good work in the world. I am very happy to be here with you.

I have just a few ideas that I want to share with you. I try to think of myself as someone who learns from my mistakes. Do you ever get the feeling that if you take that idea seriously, there is never going to be a summer vacation? That there is going to be eternal homework? Well, I want to talk about some of the homework that I have noticed for myself.

One of the first things that I think is very important for all of us who are looking to do compassionate work, looking to do peacemaking, is to keep in mind that we are not doing these good works to reform the world. We are actually doing these good works to reform our own interiors and to come closer to the Divine. This is going to have some impact on how we go about choosing our work. I suggest that each one of us choose work according to the Light that we need to unfold into our best self. Doing so, we come to our own brightest Light, that which has been divinely given us. If you look around the world today, there are all kinds of work that need doing. Sometimes in a circumstance such as ours, there are arguments about what we should do first. Very often as we talk things over, we realize that actually everything needs doing, and it all needs doing right now. I want to ask you to consider choosing work that is going to bring you to your brightest Light. As someone who has been teaching anti-burnout workshops among Friends for the last twenty years, I suggest you consider your schedule. Consider that you are looking to do your best, not your most.

The crises of the world really call for us to do our best for as long as possible. We don't need people to come tearing in and do a few fabulous things and then get tired or discouraged and go home. If you can do a small thing for a long time, that is going to be very important. So let's take a look at doing our best, and what that best looks like, and how long that best needs to go on.

You know the Biblical commandment "Love your neighbor as yourself." Our capacity to love our neighbor is diminished when we don't do a good job of loving ourselves. So maybe when that concept was put forth there should have been a footnote— something about having mercy for yourself. As we look at the task of peacemaking in these times when the war drums are beating so loudly and the potential for bad news is so fierce. We need to be careful with ourselves, especially given the noise of American popular culture. We need to be gentle with ourselves and sometimes this is very difficult. Maybe we didn't grow up learning it at home. But I would like to suggest to you that the more mercy that you have for yourself, the more mercy you will have for the next person. The more patience and tolerance that you have for the aspects of yourself with which you are not comfortable, the more patience you are going to have for the next person.

If you're having a hard time getting that mercy for yourself, there is a side door into it: gratitude. If you can pay attention to the things that are good in your life, the things that work well, the things that you are grateful for, you will find you have greater capacity to be merciful to yourself. And your capacity to be merciful with other people will grow, too. This is very important in all ministries, of course. I think a real test of a mature ministry is when you can do that loving, compassionate work with a fool. Of course, sometimes we ourselves are the fool who needs compassion, sometimes it's someone else.

Now, just for one very quick moment, think of that person at Quaker Meeting who just fries your butt and you wish to God that he or she would become a Baptist. You are just absolutely sure this person is not getting it. They have no place in Quakerism, and why are they in your Meeting, your church, or on your committee? God help them.

You know that your ministry is becoming mature when you understand that this person's foolishness is so much like your own, and that you then can set aside the personal insults, conflict, and misunderstanding. All of which gets so much more immediate when there is urgency. Set that aside and do your compassionate work. It doesn't mean you have to stop thinking they're a fool. But you do that compassionate work for that person at these Meetings. That is a lovely test as to whether or not you are going in the Light—especially during hard work.

There is a difficulty with Grace and Light in that they tend to be unscheduled events. Yet, sometimes when we are seeking Light and sometimes when we are looking for those moments of Grace, they seem just outrageously elusive. We can't schedule them. We can't steer them. We can't demand them.

However, there are some spiritual disciplines that we can practice that keep our spiritual muscles toned so we will be listening and receptive when the blessings of Grace and Light come. Those disciplines are extremely individual, and I would ask you to keep track of those things that bring you down to center, that renew your best self—those practices that honor you most. I encourage you to work them into a daily practice so you can participate in the discipline that early Friends spoke of—of leaving the meeting house on First Day, but not leaving Meeting for Worship. Don't let the noise of the world take away that ongoing contact with the Divine.

I would also like to suggest that we pay close attention to both fear and humor. As you are doing hard work out in the world, you want to be watching to see if you have chosen some work that frightens you and to what extent and how it frightens you. I think that a little bit of fear is good to sharpen the senses and make you pay good attention. But too much fear, of course, is difficult to work with. It can be difficult to follow the Light. So watch the work that you choose and find that level of fear appropriate for you, and watch for the amount of humor you bring into a situation.

Are there difficult things that you can laugh at? Chances are if you can laugh at them, it means that you have found a capacity to carry the difficulties with you as you consider and try to understand them. If there is conflict for which you have no humor at all and cannot bear humor, it probably means that you don't have the capacity to do this work gracefully.

The same is true of pain. I think we want to be absolutely fluent and literate in understanding our own pain, the pain of our lives. The better our understanding of the pain within ourselves, the more we can reach more deeply to help other people with their pain and the pain of conflict in community, at home, and internationally. So, what do you know about your own pain, what clarity do you have about the homework that you have gotten done, and what are the things that you're still sorting out?

Another piece is eccentricity. Quakers are a little bit famous for being eccentric. Perhaps, it is part of our English heritage. In my Italian family, we had some eccentrics. I had a Great Aunt Ruby who went with her friend, Suzie, to a laundromat. They had five bushels of eggplants that they needed to press water out of, but they didn't have enough crockery, so they put it on a rinse and spin cycle. I want you to pay close attention to your eccentricities, especially in difficult situations. If you are going to be the one carrying water to a large fire doing hard work in risky places, there are going to be some little things peculiar to you that are going to help you. They are going to be very individual and they are going to be unique. And, by God, I want you to claim them and I want you to keep them.

For example, I have worked with many, many women who have had sexual assaults, and I have gone into prisons to teach massage to rapists. But I make it a very firm rule never to get more than five miles away from the nearest French fry. If I can have fries, you can send me wherever you need me to go. Be very aware of your eccentricities and what it is that is peculiar to you that you need to do your work, and don't be ashamed of it.

Lastly, I want to talk a little bit about the concept of role models. There is subtlety in spirituality; it might be that the person who has the largest, strongest Light at work in them might actually be the least obvious person. It might be so subtle that you don't even know the power and the force that's coming through. I think this is particularly true of our older Friends. So I want to talk just a little bit about what I call "schlepping the Light."

Quakerism is a little bit like marriage. It takes a long time. You can be in a marriage seven years and still be at the beginning—at the beginning of unpacking, settling in, and getting to know one another. I have been a Quaker now for over thirty-five years, and I feel like I am just settling into hitting paydirt. In the beginning, it feels like true love. There is this excitement. There is this Light, and it is intoxicating and it makes you giddy and you get out there and it is just fabulous. Ah, to be a Quaker in the Light. Ah, to go and make some good Godly trouble. It's the biggest best blind date there is.

Yet, after a time—as we do our work, as we come to understand the work and the pain of the world, of loving ourselves, of loving our neighbors, of loving the fools, and all of that—it's less intoxicating, it's not as exciting, and yet it's still stunning. So there are some Friends among us who have integrated the Light more into their lives. I'm not saying that it is easy for them to carry the Light, and I'm not saying that they carry the Light more consistently, but if you look carefully among us, you will see some Friends in whom the Light is more integrated. It is not dramatic. It is not showy. I think of that as "schlepping the Light." They are carrying this brightness, this divine gift, in a way that is simple and elegant and absolutely necessary. I would ask you to watch for that, so we can all learn from it.

# Five Years in Solitary

*11/22/2003*

The work with him on Wednesday revealed the nature of what was needed and how we would proceed. I had heard that he'd been imprisoned in solitary confinement for five years in Nepal. Two of the sessions were in his college dorm room.

The first session we worked very slowly. We talked a bit. I asked him about his health currently but didn't delve into the past. I listened for what his body was saying to me. For a short time, we sat facing each other in desk chairs. I did energy work on him without touching him to be sure I could read his body and to move cautiously so as not to disturb him or cause any sense of trespass. Then I did some gentle hands-on work on his upper back and shoulders as he sat in the chair. Then, I took off the sock and shoe of one foot at a time. I did massage and energy work on his feet. I did not massage deeply, but gently and rocked each foot by laying it on my thigh, held it gently, and slowly rocked my body in the slightest gentlest way so as to imitate the subtle rocking that puts a baby to sleep. He found this relaxing. We had discussed some of his post-traumatic stress disorder symptoms beforehand. I was determined to make this as safe as possible.

For the second visit, he was very eager for the work, happy to see me, and related that his body was much more relaxed, even though his mind still raced. He wanted to know how we were going to get at his mind to slow it down. I said we would use the body to sneak up on his mind, which made him laugh—thank goodness. In this second session I asked him to lie down on his bed. I did some opening work in the air and then some general touch, then settled on working on his back. He was lying on his side so his whole back was open to me. Often the back is a good boney place to work, as it is very protected and doesn't feel vulnerable as would say the throat or the belly or the face. My hands anchored in at his sacrum and between the scapulae. There was some need in other places but mostly this is where he needed to receive truckloads of good energy for comfort, deep relaxation, and assurance that his solitary confinement was indeed over. He was with people again and could join them in doing life fully, even though he had been released ten years before.

With the third session I again asked about his health but also asked him where on his body he had been hurt while in prison. I'd assumed physical torture, but there had been none. Instead, he revealed that from the time he was twenty-two, he had spent the better part of five years in solitary confinement—two years in an underground cell without light. He had been told he'd be there for life. Throughout the third session, I worked exclusively on his back as it became clear that this was the place where he would be able to receive the major benefit.

I could do the feet, the head, and other parts, which would help, but the best place to take care of need was his back. His biggest need was to have the feeling that he was again amidst people. In his experience, the sense of being alone and adrift in the dark was so complete. The darkness could be made less by the comfort of having warm, calm touch. I needed to stay firmly and a long time in one place. This enabled his body to feel and soak in the sensation of being touched physically. He needed to receive and recover all that time devoid of any touch, of any receiving. That was my work.

# What is It and Where Does It Come From?

A friend asks: "This healing you do. What is it and where does it come from?"

Over the years I've thought of the gift of healing in different ways. At first I was stunned by the whole experience—being taken by an overwhelming feeling of compassion, nearly reduced to tears, feeling my hands grow warm and having an idea where they should be placed, and a growing sense that a good change was happening. At first I thought of this as the work of the "Holy Spirit." Being raised Catholic, what else could I think? And I came to think of it as a spiritual gift, not a talent or skill to be learned.

Later, at times when I wasn't doing the work, I would wonder why I had put this phenomenon in a spiritual frame. Couldn't it just be something peculiar about me? Maybe an illusion? Maybe a brain tumor or too much magnesium in my blood? Perhaps I'm hypnotizing myself and others. Am I just a sugar pill made up of false beliefs? All this I would sit with and ponder. Then the experience would come to teach me again, poor student that I am, what this is and where it comes from. While I am do healing work, I feel guidance and the presence of a Divine phenomenon for which I am only a conduit.

I am not in a position to decide outcome, and it is not my choice who I can and cannot help or to what degree. Here is a common situation. I come into a room to teach, and out of fifty strangers I might have deep and tender feelings for a few of them. I have some idea about the nature of their pain, how it's layered in their bodies, and how it might be moved. In the course of my teaching, I may speak with them or place my hands on them or simply stand near and feel the energy moving between us. I feel a change and they do also.

Someone once asked if this transaction depended on the depth of my faith. It would seem so. On the other hand, I can assure you that if the work depended on my perfection, very little would get done. In fact, it's just the opposite. At first, I don't feel deep faith and then the work flows out of me. I feel deep compassion and heat running through me with a sense of where it is to be directed. I follow this guidance and experience a washing of myself and this person to the extent that all pain, worry, and obstruction to love is wiped away for a time. Over and over this happens, and my faith deepens. I'm not the driver. I'm surrendering to the ride.

Sometimes I receive a message about someone's pain but am told it's not my work to do or it's not the right time or it's obstructed in some way. Sometimes it simply doesn't work and I don't understand how or why. But mostly, when I feel a flood of Light, kindness, and heat, good things happen, large and small.

My gift seems to be limited to recognizing and releasing the pain that follows trauma. I don't seem to have a gift to change tissue or disease, unlike some healers. I'm working with outer layers of energy surrounding the body. Whether this limit will shift or why, I haven't a clue. I'm just trying to attend to my experience and to be of help. If the person I'm working on perceives other types of healing, as sometimes happens, I rarely have any awareness of that.

If a healer has a sense about the source of his or her healing, hooray and many blessings on all they do! But when that sense of origin is used in some way that does not honor all, then specific labeling and naming no longer anchor a work to goodness. I've become more deliberate and careful about naming sources of this experience. I rarely use the word God any longer, as it has such terrible manipulation, violent history, and ungodly limitations placed upon it. When God is mentioned to justify war or pain, you know faith and reason have been left behind. I might say the Divine or leave the space open without naming. I think the tone one works in and the capacity to leave ego and certainty behind are more important than attaching the experience of healing to any particular named source.

In working with Christians, I've experienced the presence of Jesus and Mary. When working with Buddhists, I've experienced the presence of the Buddha. I am experiencing their faith, the frame where they understand spiritual life happens. Faith, goodness, and compassion do not come under one brand name.

There is the temptation to think of this kind of work as special or specially chosen. I can only say that if you do healing work for thirty years, that feeling of being special can shift into something different—perhaps feeling too busy and feeling needful of every possible discipline that brings rest and solitude. The genuine specialness we feel is the increase of reverence and being part of creating balance where there was hurt. My focus remains on doing my best for the long haul, and the haul is very long. No one is honored by my exhaustion or my doing too much. It is a blessing and a gift when I do my work well and learn to stay close to my best. Feeling special may be the honeymoon part of the work—it's not the feeling of the mature energy worker who listens closely and witnesses much on a path that only goes forward to show more of everything.

So, what is the healing and where does it come from? Language will always disappoint and be insufficient in spiritual matters. I think of it as Light. My sense is that it comes from the sky, the Divine, the earth, and realms we don't have names for. I believe it is and has always been a stream we can choose to step into and be part of, if we don't let the noise of modern life render us unable to respond to this invitation to intimacy with the wounded and the Divine.

# Still Learning

*January 2000*

My education on healing from trauma is an incomplete, ongoing work, which I find continually fascinating and best suited to wondering about rather than collecting hard facts about. There are so many parts to consider: life itself hurts; trouble must not only be survived, but learned about; the world seems to know no bounds in its beauty or its inhospitality.

When I began my seeking in this field, I was a teacher of young children. My talent as a teacher lay in my curiosity and my passion to create a safe space for the children who were having difficulty, most often with emotional hurt. In ten years I learned that different people need different approaches in order to receive help. The chaos of anger, shame, distrust, and expression of need is extremely individual and calls for the most careful and reverent observation. Reverent observation is a trait so absent in American cultural life that the only remedy may be vigorous self-training.

What is safe for each person is also very individual. How much physical closeness will they allow, what kind of guidance and how much can they accept, how willing are they to respond to questions or disclose information about themselves, and what can be offered and taken in—all vary from individual to individual.

After working with children, I brought my seeking to women who had been sexually assaulted. I think they are, in all likelihood, the largest group of hurt people on the planet. This is where I began to understand that hurt is layered within the person, body, and mind, depending on several changing factors. What was their understanding of their own personal power before the trauma? Was the trauma a single event, a series of events, or a situation of continual hurt? Did it happen in secret? What is their understanding of the nature of the trauma with regards to personal responsibility or current outcome? Most important, what is their understanding of their own goodness? And by this, I do not mean self-esteem, but rather the clear sense of one's essence and capacity for goodness in the world, including, perhaps, Divine connection.

While working with women I began my own healing work as someone who was raped and beaten as a young child. The deep spiritual work of going inward and outward simultaneously, to hear what there was to learn in the world and to hear what there was to learn within my own divine dialogue, became an important and regular practice.

As I expanded my seeking to the realms of people with life-threatening diseases (primarily AIDS), refugees who had been tortured, and ritual abuse survivors, the opportunity came to develop various ways to deliver calm to the distressed and retain my own inner balance. These have become the basis of workshops I have been teaching for the past eighteen years on healing from trauma and spiritual disciplines for avoiding exhaustion.

I have found that developing, maintaining, and delivering calm as a regular work is a large and difficult task. There are so many other feelings that need expression—grief, anger, fear, love, joy, and desire. Yet it's calm that is going to create enough space to allow learning following trauma. Healing from trauma is essentially sacred learning, learning which one does in awe and uncertainty.

For people wanting to join this vigil to witness hurt and its healing, I encourage that they do their own inner work, to become more conscious, deliberate, and honest, especially with regard to pain. There is much wisdom that can be transferred once the inner work is accepted and regularly attended to. If it's the simple compassion of easy giving that you seek, I don't think you will find satisfaction in witnessing the consequences and needs of people in trauma. But if you enjoy complexity, questions without answers, and know or can learn to see pain that cannot be touched, then I say welcome, bring all your tools, there is much good that needs doing.

We often think of peacemaking as political and social issues, and healing as medical and mental health issues. Yet both are the lessening of pain and confusion. Needs that are met resemble justice whether in the body that receives nutrition or a minority group receiving equal rights. The laying down of weapons resembles pain relief whether it is the full night's sleep without fear or the freedom to work in one's fields to bring in the harvest rather than stay home to guard the house. While external details change and settings vary, every person who works to lessen confusion and diminish pain is working for peace and healing.

All these years later, I still feel like a beginner with more questions than answers. Some days there's too much doubt and not enough strength in all its various forms. I want to be a better student. I want to have more faith and discipline. I am also grateful that I am on the spiritual adventure of my life.

# Surrender Over and Over

*October 1995*

This afternoon I worked with a young woman recovering from ritual abuse. How such hurt can be survived is itself a miracle. She felt that she had no soul. She only barely and with great effort has a life beyond her pain. I do not repeat the ritual abuse stories. They are obscene in their reach for the inhuman. Her hurt is layered deeply. Almost as one is convinced of spiritual awakening, she has been forced into "knowing" she is vile from the core outward. Poisoned and leaking describe her self-image.

As I worked with her I surrendered over and over again to the grace of the precious moment, when one who is hurting has safe harbor for a time and someone to tell the story to. It's the blessing of time in which to unwrap the bandages for fresh air and witness, to wash the aloneness of hurt.

When I was a schoolteacher I had precious moments when a child was hurt or confused and I could bring back some sense of safety or comfort or understanding. This fed me in a way I cannot describe. I had the great joy of making trust the largest presence in a given moment. Over and over again this cleaned my interior and confirmed my sense of how life is to be given the right push, the best tone.

Now the essence of the work is the same. I am still watching for the nature of the hurt and how it lies within a person. I watch and listen to gather a sense of what's happened, what's needed, and how my gift can best be delivered. There's a kind of grace to it that relies on uncontrollable aspects. I can never know what might come of that gift. Often it helps. Sometimes it doesn't, and going forward might even hurt more. Though that's rare, it happens. Sometimes there's a feeling that as I listen to the wounded, all I can do is ask, "What's needed?" and listen for Divine guidance. I try to listen inwardly and outwardly with equal balance. What can be seen and known may change as patterns reveal themselves.

# Abandoned

"I just want you to know that I am going to have a big life transition this weekend. I'm sure your teaching will be good for the other people, but, truth be known, I organized this retreat because I need you here for me and my own changes."

She was that clear, and so over the next few days I watched to see what knots she had to untie, what hurt, what pattern deprived her of fullness. By the third day when she stood at the sink washing the morning dishes and told me she was angry and sad about having to go to work today—work she loved, work she had a talent for, helping people understand their problems—the pattern was revealed.

"Could we do some energy work?" I ask.

"Yes."

On the living room couch, her head on the pillow in my lap, she lay on her side, feet and knees drawn up a bit. I placed one hand on her head and another on her shoulder. I could feel the appetite for comfort competing with the radar of doubt that questioned the reality of help. I moved my hands to various places to rest for a bit on the jaw, the forehead, the crown, the temple, the back of the neck, the back of the head. All these helped but did not truly release the deeply held anger and sadness or reveal them clearly.

My left hand was drawn down the back. Where is it? Shoulder blades? No, there's tension there but no old hurt. Mid-back? No, only strength, fortitude, and scrappiness there. Sacrum? No, balance and grounding are clear. I placed my hand on the low back looking for the old hurt. Yes, it was there. Up a full hand from the sacrum, I placed my hand like a rope mooring a ship just in from stormy seas. She took a deeper breath and settled into the couch as though for a good sleep. I settled in knowing that I had tapped a reservoir of old hurt that could begin to be released. The radar of doubt switched off and deep relaxation displaced the frustration of the old familiar mix of anger and tears.

As her back sagged and sank into comfort, I could see in the eyes of my heart that somehow, at about five to seven years old this child became a provider, a mommy, and she had never stopped. Now she ached for receiving but had designed a life without it. She had instead polished her giving until its shine drew in the most needy.

Hands On

Over the many years she had helped so many others wash their souls of suffering and confusion that her own laundering began without raising a hand. Her own wisdom was now revealing not only her strength from old struggle, but also the losses. She had gone without for so long she just couldn't do that any longer.

Before an hour is up, I have given what I can, and we make a date for lunch when I can share what I have seen. That's when I tell her she's been the mommy too long, that she's exhausted by giving to so many and receiving from so few. Her mouth drops, and she tells of her mother abandoning her and her younger siblings when she was seven years old. I draw a chart with three columns across the top—Mommy, Peer, Baby. Along the side I list categories: lover, job, friends, family, body.

|  | **Mommy** gives only | **Peer** balanced giving and receiving | **Baby** receives only |
|---|---|---|---|
| **Lover** |  |  |  |
| **Job** |  |  |  |
| **Friends** |  |  |  |
| **Family** |  |  |  |
| **Body** |  |  |  |

Thinking of mommy as primary giver and peers as a balanced give-and-take and baby primarily as receiver, I ask her to consider each of the five relationship categories to see where in her life she gives only, gives and receives, and receives only.

She confirms the need for all the rebalancing, takes a deep breath, . . . and gazes at the horizon seeing how much work this means.

# Queries for Caregivers

Quakers often use what they call "queries" as a focus for individual and collective meditation, consideration, and prayer. These queries assist in a search for greater love, truth, and insight into how to serve humanity and how to live in accordance with core values. Queries might be self-created, group-created, or drawn up by Yearly Meetings for exploration. They are intended as questions to live with and into, not as a test to fail or pass. The following queries can be valuable whether you are a Quaker, a caregiver, or just someone seeking deeper understanding.

- What is your preparation for receiving spiritual guidance?

- Who is teaching you?

- What are your disciplines for centering?

- What is the difference between your long-term and short-term preparation?

- How do you prepare your body to make this gift?

- How do you prepare your workspace?

- Do you have material tools of the trade?

- Are there times when you are working blind? How is your trust?

- How do you track your own pain and separate it from the pain of your clients?

- Do you move in and out of grace? How well do you do that?

- What do you do with sexual energy during work?

- What is the place of money in your spiritual work? Why is that?

- What is your best mode of learning this work?

- How many levels are you listening to during work?

- Where else in your life are you listening to multiple realities?

- How do you know you are ready? Why do some clients trouble you?

- How do you define success and failure in this work? Is that trouble?

- Are pain and suffering different? Do you separate them? For whom?

- Should your own life be the largest stimulus you know?

- What kinds of clients do you learn from? What kinds don't you like ?

- What are the places where you are stuck? Who knows this?

- What are the ways you refresh, revitalize, and restore yourself?

- What hurts most in you?

- What is your ideal work situation?

- What are the more famous lessons you've been learning?

- What's changed in your two lists of figured out/not figured out?

- Is the care you bring to others similar to the care you bring yourself?

# Healing Notes

*December 1993*

The first work is always to ask God, Yahweh, the Holy Spirit—whatever words mean the Great Mystery for you—to be with you now. And for you to demonstrate the calm and grace that comes with that Presence so the ones you are to help can see and feel that even though you clearly see their pain, your peace and calm remains firm and large. You see their hurt and know it. You feel how it is akin to your own and how it is different. You feel how it has patterns and is fought or accepted, deep or shallow, engaged or feared.

Sometimes the Spirit moves me to release the pain. This happens more often than not. The not times were hard to accept at first, as if it were my own failure of strength or concentration, but I have learned this is not so. In my worst possible shape—tired, angry, sick, hung over, despairing, mean, blaming—I have handed myself over to be used and holy work has been done. Not by me of course, but by the Holy Spirit using me. It seems as though there's a great plan, and I can have a part at times. The why or when I can help and the why or when I can't is mere speculation. That is my sense of it. So I must accept pain as well as its release as a part of life.

I help people to work with the pain and not lose heart, or hope, or joy. I help give pain a place where it is not overwhelming, but becomes a companion. I think this is an essence of life, one we know when there is reverence in our hearts and minds. When we move without reverence, or any sense of the holy, we lose the idea that pain and joy have their places. We must embrace them and work with them each moment to keep each awake and in balance.

# Section 5

## Healing Trauma

The Nature of Trauma       109

The Nature of Healing       115

Gracefulness       119

Making Space for Choice       126

Three Friends       130

Giving, Exhaustion, and Despair       133

Living Through Grace, Living on Gifts       140

# The Nature of Trauma

Typically we think of balance as staying centered so we don't tip over—stand on one leg and don't lean too far forward or back or to the side or you'll fall. That's one idea of balance.

Another way of looking at balance is going far out to the edge from the center and returning, then going far out again to another edge and returning. Out and back, over and over again. That's a kind of balance, also. It has rhythm and movement. We go somewhere and then return to a known place. This kind of balance helps us manage the everyday extremes of life. We are alone, then we are with many people. We are in a quiet place, then we are in a noisy place. We are in love and open hearted, then not. We work, then rest. We are in motion and then still. As we go through life there's a rhythm we develop in order to move smoothly from one small extreme to the next. This kind of balance helps us get to work on the hard days. It helps us shift gears for the unexpected delight or problem. It's a way of knowing how to walk in our own world on regular days.

Trauma is any event or situation that deeply changes in a negative way how we feel about being in the world. Suddenly, what it means for us to be here in the world is not as good a deal as we thought it was before the trauma. Something essential has changed, and it doesn't look good, not now and not as far as we can see. We can no longer get back from the edge as we did before with ease and grace. Trauma changes all the ways we are in the world—moving, sleeping, eating, socializing, planning, working, loving, problem-solving. It changes everything because the world is no longer what we thought it was. Trauma makes everything feel different, including sometimes no longer trusting our own senses.

There are two qualities common to all trauma: abruptness and the sense of events being surreal or incredible.

Abruptness is a sense of BOOM! like a bomb's gone off. This can be deceptive because the traumatic experience itself may not be immediate in terms of time—perhaps something like recalling long-term child abuse happening at regular intervals. Yet the experience of our pain comes to us abruptly when we realize how much pain we feel. When the change in reality is caused by the memory of being hurt long ago, there can still be a feeling of immediacy because that's how it comes into our awareness. Whether the abruptness is in the traumatic event itself or not, we experience it that way because the recall or awareness always hits like a ton of bricks. Our response is likewise abrupt. Even when it's the expected news from the doctor saying, "Yes, it's inoperable," there is no way we can completely prepare for that moment.

The sense of events being surreal or incredible is always a part of us that can't believe this thing is really happening, a feeling that this is not possible. We have some idea that other people will have a turn at feeling the worst, but it's a shock when we see trauma being delivered with our name on it.

These two qualities of feeling abruptness and surrealism tend to frame our common response to trauma: *contraction*. To regain some control following trauma, we begin to pull in and make ourselves, our world, and our experience smaller. This happens at three distinct levels: in our physical bodies, in the ways we think, and in our emotional repertoire. The contraction serves two purposes. The first is to protect us should the trauma recur, the monsters return. The second is to organize some numbness so as not to feel all our pain all the time. To attempt to feel all our feelings 100% of the time following trauma would be to court madness. Contraction affects our bodies, thoughts, and emotions.

*The Body*

Our bodies are not easily contracted or numbed. It takes a great deal of effort to hold one's body in a smaller shape and keep it there. It also takes much effort and concentration to organize and maintain numbness, to not feel the hurt. It's tiring. And yet this is common response in our bodies following traumatic experience.

Think of a dancer—the upright posture of a standing person, head up, eyes on the far horizon, chest out, legs firmly held with weight evenly distributed, ready for motion. Now think of the posture of one who has come to the end of a hard week of work with much overtime and no break in sight because so much remains to be done. Tension, exhaustion, and the last remaining wisps of hope combine for a very different posture. The head is pushed forward and hung down, creating a curve at the top of the spine. The legs shuffle slowly without momentum. Now combine this with the image of a dog that realizes it's losing the fight and it's now time to leave, quickly. Think of how far that tail is tucked, causing the entire pelvis to tilt so as to slant the backside under and in. This creates a curve at the other end of the spine.

It is common following trauma for the body to begin to contract, causing a C-curve in the spine. The head comes forward and down to protect the heart. The shoulders have a sense of bearing the weight of the world. The pelvis is curved in and under from the back completing the C-curve. This effectively makes the body smaller, making it feel less vulnerable to attack from the monsters outside.

There's also protection from the monsters inside in the way of numbness. Unexpressed anger, sadness, and fear are generally stored in the solar plexus, a bundle of nerves at the top of the belly. We store these large and difficult feelings so we can make an inventory of damages later at a slower, more controlled rate. Unlike the monsters from the outside, these monsters are on the inside. They can set off an avalanche of true emotion that replays the trauma, so they must be tucked in. Keeping these feelings tucked in can restore a sense of balance, of control. It is an automatic, unconscious use of storage common to all trauma.

The C-curve in our posture helps to lock the feelings in storage and quiet down the tumult. An upright posture tends to allow these feelings to be more accessible to the heart area, where they can be deeply experienced, and up to the head where they can be expressed.

The contraction extends to other parts of the body. There tends to be a general increase in muscle soreness and stiffness simply because our entire body is constantly being held more tightly. Our capacity for deep relaxation is there, but the effort at our core levels becomes focused on surviving—avoiding further attack and controlling pain with as much numbness as can be organized. Until we use relaxation deliberately, we tend to put all of our effort into the automatic crisis mode: "Keep going! Don't think back! Don't look down! Don't cry!" It's as if we are attempting to leave our bodies and the known trauma physically.

*Our Thoughts*

As we go through life, we develop many assumptions about what it means to be here. We have ideas about what's hard, what we know about, what's easy, what we must be careful with, and the list can be endless. Many of these ideas are unspoken and even unconscious. Generally, they serve us well, until the monster of trauma shows up. Then much of what we have assumed doesn't hold up. In the war zone of traumatic experience, much of what we held to be true in peace time can no longer be relied on. So, big questions come up: Is there such a thing as credible love, and if so why do I feel so isolated and unreachable now? Is there such a thing as safety for anyone anywhere, and if so why can't I feel that even as a possibility? Is there such a thing as a balance between good and evil, and why has all this pain come to me? Why me? Why now? Haven't I been a good person?

Many of these ideas are unconscious, or at least unspoken, and we leave them that way. This is why it's common to see people survive a traumatic experience and move into a miserly posture with their life, to take on a philosophy of scarcity. Reliable safety, credible love, and a sense of balance all have been struck a blow. And it seems logical this changes what it means to be alive forever. There seems to be less of everything to work with and what we have can't be counted on to stay—that's the perception.

This is the contracted thinking that goes on following trauma. Considering new ideas is really contrary to the contraction that's going on in the mind. There is a tendency to reach for what is familiar whether or not it honors us. It's the reach for comfort rather than getting well, a return to the familiar known and away from further uncertainty. Taking in new ideas is an expansive gesture, the opposite of circling the wagons and holing up for the duration. This contraction limits the possibilities for responding to crisis. It means that our appetite for trying new ways of being, engaging new patterns of doing life, might feel like a further intrusion into what has already caused too much motion or change.

*Emotion*

Our emotional life is probably the most obvious place to look for contractions after the monsters visit. Our capacity to feel and express is constricted by the desire to hurt less, to appear less crazy than we feel, and to avoid any further drift away from the familiar. In other words, if we don't feel it, it may not be so or it may be less so.

This contraction of the emotional repertoire tends to reveal itself as a strong resistance to feel and express emotions, which often shows up in three ways:

- Inability or unwillingness to make expressions of personal power

Healing Trauma

- Resistance to receiving love deeply

- A diminished capacity to recognize and make choices

The traumatized have difficulty saying, "STOP THAT, YOU'RE HURTING ME!" or "I NEED THIS FROM YOU!" They are expressions of personal power outside the contracted emotional repertoire. Such expressions of personal power are large things that take energy and movement and certainty. All these are in short supply if you are just trying to get through the next few moments or the day.

There are two reasons such feelings are difficult to express. First, people immediately tend to blame themselves for pain. This seems to be an automatic design flaw in human beings. As soon as the shit hits the fan in someone's life, doubt looms large, and the idea takes over that one would not be in this trouble if one hadn't been careless, or stupid, or willful, or so much like one always is. If we blame ourselves for all our own troubles, we don't feel worthy of help or relief. We believe that we are not entitled to feel better because it's all our own fault anyway.

Second, it takes a great deal of energy to maintain contraction. If we are using all our might just to get through the day, we simply don't have the spare energy to make expressions of personal power. If we spend each and every day keeping our hands clenched in a fist, we have less energy to sing, run, or make sense. It's a major act of expanding the self to express personal power without trauma; following trauma, it's not only like swimming upstream, but doing so backwards wearing weight belts.

When we come to believe that love and goodness are illusions, we become unable to let others take care of us and less able to take care of ourselves. The doors and windows that we shut and lock to keep the monsters out are the same doors and windows that let our goodies in. Receiving love deeply means opening those doors and windows, which might disturb our efforts at monster protection and numbness. *Might.* Curiously, after the monster shows up there is a often a tendency to assume that all news is bad news, that the next phone call or conversation will only make things worse.

Similarly, we believe we cannot let down our guard without being clobbered by our own feelings. If we allow ourselves to receive care deeply, won't we feel the tremendous burn of pain that we have just worked so hard to store in numbness? If we open ourselves to feeling what it is we need, won't there be an avalanche of need coming forward from a storehouse of disappointment?

How can we take in some of what we need without ruining our defenses? All this complex of doubt and fear sets up a perfectly logical resistance to receive love deeply. Yes, perhaps we can take in a bit and be grateful for moments. But deeply? No thanks, too much possibility for hurt.

The belief in keeping the doors barricaded can be held so fiercely that no improvement can even be considered possible without risking grave danger. No other reality exists in this state.

Given these perceptions, our capacity to recognize and make choices is diminished. Caught up in protecting ourselves from the possibility of further trauma, we are unable to stand back, take in the big picture, and see what our choices and options might be. We can't see the big picture because we are so busy squinting to keep from seeing anything else frightening. New possibilities are totally contrary to the contraction of body, mind, and spirit in reaction to trauma. Our capacity for shortened vision cannot be underestimated following trauma. Feelings? What feelings? There are always more choices than we can see. The broader our vision, the more possibilities come into view. The more contracted our idea of life is, the fewer the choices that can be seen. If there is one aspect of life that makes for more madness than all others, it is probably the absence of choice in how we view our lives. Whether we are responding to something outward or inward, the aspect of choice and how we perceive that range is critical to how our ride in this life will feel.

This is what I have come to know of the nature of trauma from my experiences in working with the traumatized.

# The Nature of Healing

Healing is a very old word from a Greek root which means to bring all the pieces together again as they were before. A small cut that heals entirely, for example; there might be blood, then a bit of a scab, but by and by the skin comes together, often leaving no scar. That's the original idea.

When it comes to recovery from trauma, this kind of healing is not possible. The pieces do not go back together again the way they were before. What we have seen and felt is ours, and we can't make that disappear. We have to expand our understanding of healing to include the realities of recovery from trauma. At its best, healing from trauma is learning to move pain and suffering into wisdom and knowledge. It's not making the horror disappear quickly so much as seeing the photograph of our life's pain fade and fade and fade. We come to the place where the learning is never forgotten, but we are not stuck organizing our whole life, moment to moment, around our pain.

There are two very present elements in the work of healing from trauma. One is fear. Such a well known aspect of life hardly needs any introduction at all. Fear is something that we learn as we go through life, get hurt, and become afraid that we'll be hurt again. It's loud and aggressive. It can be heard in people's voices frequently. It's learned. Fear is not original equipment. We don't start out with fear, but it is in charge of the motivation and organization of the contraction. It says:

"You see! I told you there were monsters out there but you didn't listen to me. Now look at the mess we're in! I'm in charge now and there are going to be a lot of rules! We're not going out at night! We're going to sit up and fold our hands! And no laughing!"

That's fear—pushy, in control, certain of the worst, logical though narrow, and lousy company. Fear is so common in our culture that it has lost its place as spice and pretends to be a main dish.

There is also hope, another old word and a very particular idea, an idea in our culture that is often confused with wishing. People will say, "Oh, I hope I win the lottery." That's wishing. The original idea of hope is this—the desire for goodness with the expectation that it can be achieved. That's exact. In other words, "I need some improvement here, and I think I can get it if I . . . " That's hope— the belief in the possibility that it can get better, and we can have a hand in making it happen. Hope is organic. We don't learn it. We have it when we are born. The child turning to suckle is not committing an idle act of being. It is the desire to thrive. Children coming into a classroom with a huge appetite to know the names of things and how things work exhibit a desire to thrive and be in the world. These are acts of hope. Hope is very strong in children. You may have noticed that young children are shocked when an adult is being horrible. They have very little idea why anyone would be so awful. And they are so full of hope that an adult has to be horrible on a regular basis for children to write them off.

Also, hope is a passion. This is wonderful because it means that hope is very strong. We can rely on it as a lever to boost our way along difficult paths. It's what makes people able to do the impossible every day. It is not always easy to reach hope. It can get covered over with pain and fatigue. But I am certain that each person has the hope they need to do their work. I have seen it again and again.

Hope has a very specific role in healing. For every person who is looking to get well, there is a dance between hope and fear. The dance looks something like this. We are doing regular life. A monster appears, and we are hurt. Fear grabs hold of the steering wheel of our life and lays down all kinds of rules setting into place a contraction, a compression of our former life. Our ways of thinking become smaller, our bodies become constrained, and our emotions are less free. After a time, hope comes out and says, "Now fear, I understand why you are doing all this. I saw the monster too, and I know there were damages. But you have made life so small in here that I am bored to tears. This is not living. Can we draw the drapes? Get some fresh air? Can we call a friend? Go for a walk? See a movie? Have some ice cream? I need a little something in here. Could we just come out from under the futon and stop screaming for five minutes?" That's the job of hope, to lobby in the legislature of the heart for space to make choice.

Hope is very wise. It does not push all the time, and it does not nag. It comes to challenge fear and rattle the armor and when it is a good time for change. That is why the healing of trauma is cyclical. No one does the work all at once or all the time. There's a cycle to it. The monster shows up and there's hurt, then the beginning of contraction. We take some initial actions then we rest and protect. By and by the time comes round again to take another inventory of the damages, make some decisions, take some actions, and then we rest again.

Healing Trauma

The cycle is extremely individual. The period of taking action before retreating into rest can go on and on for months or years or may be only a matter of moments. There is much support for this phase generally because we assume it's a sign of health to be active and taking on the homework of getting well by movement and visible effort. The period of rest when no new information or challenge can be taken on with one's best effort is also an extremely variable component of one's life. We must bear in mind that while our culture applauds hard work, it gives almost no regard to one's capacity to rest. This results in many people having no idea of how tired they are. And for those of us healing from trauma it means this part of our organic cycle is often confused with denial and is condemned. We must have respect for the time of rest. Just as we support the efforts of those among us who strive to reach their farthest, we must support and acknowledge the integrity of the time when it is wise to lie down and restore the mind, body, and emotional life with stillness, calm, and peacefulness. Both work and rest are important and necessary. Both have a role to play and balance one another.

There is the problem of denial. Denial occurs when someone does not recognize his or her wounds or the need for healing work. We must not confuse this with resting, when someone knows that much work lies ahead but for now it's time to rest. One need for rest is that the world can be brutally inhospitable. Too often people are late in beginning large work simply because of the inhospitality of the world.

The largest and hardest aspects of healing take place when there are two points of energy existing at the same time. That's when we have big change. One is a point of energy external to us and is a source of some comfort or control or reason for hope. This might be a therapeutic relationship, a work of art, Divine intervention, a safe place, or a regular time of quiet. Another is the point of extra energy within ourselves, which is the extra energy needed to find a resource that has something to offer, to trust it, to reach out, get what's needed, and to receive it deeply. This is totally contrary to the contraction and takes much energy to head in exactly the opposite direction—outward, expansive. It's when these two points come together simultaneously that we are capable of large change.

There is a tendency in our culture to rank pain. We line up all the hurts one can have and grade them by what we think is their degree of horror. Having a migraine goes above stubbing your toe but below getting a divorce, which is below terminal illness, and so forth. But if we want to truly understand the situation, we must look beyond how the pain looks to an outsider; we have to consider how a person experiences the pain and responds to it. Our assumptions of who can bear what and with what losses are often wrong.

All pain is remarkably similar, yet two variables are at work— the nature of the pain experienced and our response to that pain. If the trauma has been a singular brief event such as surviving a terrifying car crash without injuries, then our experience of it is very different from say abduction and torture over several months. The pain resulting from a half hour sexual assault has a different effect than sexual abuse in secret in a series of events over years. The longer the period of feeling out of control and at the mercy of ongoing hurt, the deeper the damage to our sense of what it means to be in the world.

Our life experience before the monster arrived also influences how we experience and respond to trauma. If we had some sense of our own power and a clear feeling of welcome in the world before, then we may have more sense of choice and recovery. Those who encounter hurt very early on in life, may have precious little to draw on. This make childhood trauma so difficult to heal. To understand someone's pain from trauma I want to know:

- Was this a singular event or a series of hurts?
- Did this hurt happen in secret?
- How old was this person at the time of the trauma?
- Did the child have a sense of personal power before the hurt?

# Gracefulness

The work of healing from trauma calls for many skills and much learning. It tends to be a long path with places of rest and work, comfort and pain, difficulty and easiness all braided in. All these conditions call for a student and gymnast more than a warrior, though the need for bravery is great. More than all else, there is the need to be graceful, not bump into things and add to the pain and confusion of trauma. We seek a balance of what is needed to make it the best journey.

There is a set of disciplines for making the journey graceful. They help us keep our balance, come back to center, shrug off confusion, and maintain focus on where we are headed no matter the storm. If we are going to deal with a monster, our own or someone else's, let's prepare now for the hard part so we will be ready beforehand.

The monsters distort our lives in very particular ways. They make us forget our essence, our core sense of who we are. They spread a reality portraying life as only burden, no joy or sunshine. And they drain us of strength and balance. Be it terror, physical pain, overwhelming grief, or some combination of these, the monsters create the appearance of life without hope, with no good choices or possibility for change.

Three disciplines of gracefulness help us keep our essence, our balance, and our understanding that life, even when it is hard, is beautiful. They allow us to make our way where no way is apparent. They help to restore our deepest knowledge of ourselves. They are: commitment to joy, awareness, and self-discipline. Movements and actions, not just ideas, these disciplines are tools that enable us to loosen the monster's grip and pull us toward our best selves.

## A Commitment to Joy

Joy is the balance to sadness. Too much of either is an imbalance that can hurt. To get stuck in one or the other is not to feel life but an unreal corner of life. A commitment to joy is used to balance the surplus of sadness following trauma. It's a decision to know and call upon those things that remind us that life is good. We have reminders constantly that life is hard. So we make a commitment to joy to strive for balance.

Each of us has things that make us glad to be in the world, that make us feel full of life and awake. We want to know what those things are and bring more of them into our life. These bring us to our best selves, instill gratitude, and remind us that the juiciness of life is important. We want to be aware of what those things are for each of us and be deliberately reaching for them as we go through each day. We also want to be aware of what does *not* honor us, what does *not* bring us to our best, and begin to lay those things down. It's the spring cleaning of our lives. Out with the nasty—the obstacles to our best—and in with more of what honors us. This is the commitment to joy.

The music we listen to, the people we spend time with, the colors we surround ourselves with, all are messages we give to ourselves about how we feel about being in the world. If you send yourself good messages, it will be easier to meet challenges and take on hard work. If you send yourself messages that do not honor your best, doing hard work becomes harder.

We're not talking about perfection here. We're talking about moving in the direction we want to go. The commitment to joy is not a place or static thing, but a movement toward. It's not about being happy all the time and insisting that life is always and only beautiful. It's about knowing what is good and beautiful, so when the sight of the worst pain fills our eyes, we can still know a balance of life. It's not to use joy to deny or mask pain, but to be able to be with pain and not mistake it for all of reality.

What makes you glad to be here? Know what those things are. Know the familiar things, and find new ones. What is around that does not bring you to your best self and dishonors that best? Start laying those things down and keep track of that list, too.

*A Commitment to Awareness*

A commitment to awareness is another discipline of gracefulness. What we can know with all our senses and what we can feel in ways that we don't even have ways to describe yet are the total picture of our awareness. To do the hard work of getting well, of hanging out with the monsters, we want to know as clearly as possible all there is to be aware of in our situation. Trauma has lots of trapdoors, mazes, and switchbacks that can confuse and bewilder us, sometimes suddenly and without warning. A commitment to awareness is to decide to seek clearness all along the path. Confusion can add to pain and prolong suffering if we allow control without limits. We may simply need to recognize we're momentarily confused.

There are two layers of awareness to engage. One is the long term historical one of our lives. The other is the immediate right now, this moment. We want to know what we are bringing to a situation from a lifetime of experience and also to know about the current tides and gravities of a situation.

Let's take a look at our lives like a big book we've been writing. Go over the chapters. Where have we been? What have we seen? What is the emotional landscape of our journey to now? What have we learned along the way that is still true? Dare to go over the whole story, not just the most recent events.

We have all gotten this far, and that has been a major achievement for many of us. I know there were several times we almost didn't make it this far. But we did, and so we know lots. We know about all kinds of things that have allowed us to manage life for this long. What is it we know then from having come this far?

This long view informs us about what we do and don't bring to our healing work. If you have had a previous encounter with something, you may have some ideas about how to move or not move on it this time. Our own history is a checklist for the wisdom we have acquired that can be transferred into another situation. By reviewing our history we have more confidence about what we already know. This confidence encourages us when we feel lost. It also frames what we don't know.

Knowing that you don't know is a luxury. It means we know we need help before we start. It might mean we can set this work aside for now until there is more information or a better idea of what's needed.

We also need to be aware of ourselves and our situation in the present moment. How we are doing? What are we seeing this moment? What things do we sense in ourselves and those around us at this moment? Let's bring all of our listening and radar to this moment and sense what collection of life songs and noises are being played out right now, within us and around us.

In being aware of what is going on in the moment, I have found the six healing sayings useful. All of the important messages that we give one another can be arranged in categories headed by these six sayings. Each saying represents a whole body of deep feeling and embraces many expressions of those feelings. Often in the context of trauma, the feelings that are most difficult to express become impossible even to approach, let alone say out loud to another. So we want to listen to each of these six sayings and know our ability to say them as we feel them. The six sayings are:

- I love you.
- Thank you.
- I'm sorry.
- I need help.
- That's not good enough.
- NO/STOP!

These sayings are very powerful because they are essential expressions of deep feeling. Hence, they must be employed with care and respect to be aligned with truth and healing, and not used for manipulation.

Some of us grew up in homes where the power of these sayings was not permitted each person. Adults forget that children are our emotional equals. Many of us work in places where honest expression is not welcome. Our culture often derives its practice and rules for expression from structures that permit power to only a chosen few. All this can skew our ideas, understanding, and practice of saying what we mean and what we feel. Being nice and polite when we feel neither, or brutalizing others as a way of dealing with the world, can be aspects of the same power imbalance.

We change that imbalance by stretching our repertoire to include the expressions we are not at home with. We learn the use of power by trying new muscles or unused muscles. In some cases the muscles of power are overly fit, and it is the surrender reflexes that remain unused, surrender to kindness as giver or receiver, surrender to apology or forgiveness.

You can play with these six sayings to come to learn their use. First off, it's good to know which of the six are most difficult for you to use. Bring to mind someone you love, someone whose love you trust and find credible. Then go through those six sayings to see which is the easiest for you to express in any way to that person and what is the most difficult for you to express. Do we have enough understanding of our own history to see how we have come to be arranged this way? How do we feel about that arrangement? What injustice is encouraged by our not having

Healing Trauma

balance in saying what we feel? Who is hurt by our underuse or overuse of this power?

*I love you* is used to reassure when it is true and used as a manipulation when it is not true. How true this saying is varies with the speaker's and the listener's ability to be open to feeling that connection. The reality of "I love you" takes some depth in a moment of awareness. We don't always take time to feel this but merely coast through. It is the glue that holds together hope, promise, and wholeness in all different kinds of love. Without it we face despair, loneliness, and isolation unprotected.

*Thank you* is the acknowledgment of life's interdependence and a key to much balance. Without gratitude, we fail to notice what is beautiful in life and succumb to depression. Gratitude is also a doorway to mercy, a rare and valuable quality that can smooth out the impossible and bridge unfathomable breaches. Can we be grateful for even the small things that are OK and going well? Can we keep track of these to remind ourselves that all is not lost?

*I'm sorry* accepts that we all have the capacity to hurt another. Even the kindest person can bump into the most frail by accident and cause harm. It brings all of us into the family of humanity by acknowledging how balance is achieved in the surrender of pride and power for the awareness of responsibility and offended bonds.

*I need help* is the basis for our commonality. Everyone needs help of some sort. It is the common ground of human experience. It means we honestly acknowledge our reliance on others and we do not live by the illusions of independence or separateness.

*That's not good enough* declares that injustice is present. It's a statement of self-worth. It calls for recognition of elements that create oppression and their removal. This is not to be used to belittle those without power or to be mean to those who try hard and may still miss the mark.

*NO/STOP!* announces the limit of our tolerance. It says, "How dare you!" and gives notice that a trespass has occurred or is about to occur. It marks the end of patience and reserve and fair warning. It might be the spot where disrespect has begun, and further civil discourse may no longer be possible.

Can we begin by saying each of these six sayings to ourselves? Can we be honest enough with ourselves that we use these sayings to guide our next move toward more awareness and honesty about our feelings? And then use them with others?

Each of these sayings has been used to hurt people deliberately and consciously. But let us not confuse the act of taking the bread knife from the kitchen into the alley with the bread knife itself. We need to monitor our honesty and our intention in using the sayings, following traumatic experience when we may be suspicious of all use of power, and our expression of it may be crippled.

How can we possibly use something the world has put off limits and our own experience suggests will only be more hurtful? The same way my Uncle John taught me to drive. He took me to a big field where there was nothing to hit. Showed me where the brake was first and then the gas. His old truck became my introduction to the balance of gas and clutch, years before the law allowed and I actually needed the skills. So too with the expressions of power; we must find what we are least comfortable with and play with them, before we are in a tight space and need to use them instinctively. If even the suggestion of anger scares you, then begin with reminders that until these sayings can be backed up with fierce emotion, they are mere words. Experiment. Try on the expressions as if you are playing dress up. Say the most outrageous things in private and learn their flavor apart from whatever experiences made them inaccessible to you.

*A Commitment to Self-discipline and Strength*

Finally, gracefulness requires a commitment to self-discipline and strength. Staying strong in the presence of great pain is important work. Awareness and joy depend on our ability to maintain our strength especially during long stretches of hard work. So what we know about keeping our strength, renewing energy, and growing stronger within ourselves is a key to healing from trauma.

Each of us has ways to bring ourself back to center, practices that help us to lay down the noise of the world and clear our understanding. Individually we use many different things to come out of our confusion and panic, and return to the solid ground of our calm. The conscious effort to do this is the commitment to self-discipline and strength. It's vital that we find the practices that work for us and employ them on a regular basis.

The list of things that can bring us back to center is enormous. It goes from aerobics and windsailing, to prayer and meditation, to yoga and Tai Chi, to running and swimming, to gardening and

Healing Trauma

chess, to splitting firewood and playing bridge. What helps you to come back out of the pain and confusion so profuse in our world?

When we choose an activity to make a regular practice, we should watch for two things that will signify its usefulness to us. The first is that it should be cleansing. Whatever we choose should help to clear out all the entanglements, distractions, and uncertainties for a time. It should help us to feel only ourselves and restrict stimulus from an outward flow, the all too often inundation of the world.

Secondly, it should increase our concentration. Our ability to focus is the first casualty of fatigue and despair. So exercise this muscle; it will be challenged over and over. The muscle we use to be completely present and bring all of our gifts to bear on a piece of work is the same muscle we use to set aside all work no matter how nagging. What activity engages us fully, shares what is has to offer, and transforms us by separating us from work?

Whatever activities you choose, build them into a regular practice so that their benefit begins to shape and affect you. Reach for what will help balance. Use it regularly—daily, before you need it, before you are too undone by the work to reach for the calm. Over time you will become less fatigued by hard work and less worried about what you don't know, and it will be easier to maintain a balanced view of the world as both beautiful and wounded. All these bring more calm and make for better life.

Graceful discipline using these three commitments helps us move smoothly as we seek for more Light, less pain, and better understanding. Joy, awareness, and strength bring a new sense of empowerment as we use them together.

# Making Space for Choice

Part of healing trauma involves making space. We need to create space within our bodies to relax the contractions, space within our emotional life so that our feelings can be more freely expressed, and space within our thoughts to consider new choices and new ways to be in the world.

The tools for making space for choice are simple and pragmatic. They are humor, honesty, and compassion. Our goal is to watch for opportunities to invite these elements into our response to life. A new challenge arises: Can we use one of these tools to create space today, or is fear the only true gut level response we have today? That's the primary focus of making space for choice—smoothing out moment-to-moment living by deliberately incorporating elements that bring in more Light, more reason to live and enjoy life.

*Humor*

Humor has a great deal of power. It changes the body, thoughts, and emotional life by cutting through rigidity and releasing contraction. It creates space in the body by releasing contracted muscles. We can't carry something heavy and laugh deeply. When we can't resist the laughter, we have to set the heavy thing down. The diaphragm is the muscle in the top of the belly where laughter starts. It's a big strong muscle connected to the breastbone and ribs in the front, to the vertebrae in the back, and almost entirely separates the upper and lower torso. When met with laughter, it starts to roll like an ocean wave. Everything in its neighborhood is affected and becomes central to the rest of the being.

Humor creates space in the mind by expanding the playing field thoughts have to work with. Humor reminds us of this broader definition of the self. We are always more than the worst that is happening to us. What can we laugh at amidst a sea of problems? Sometimes we can laugh at ourselves. To make fun of our own troubles introduces the element of detachment, the idea that we know we are not only our pain or our problems but much more than that. Detachment can be more easily learned through humor.

Humor's best gift to the emotional repertoire is to challenge fear. When we can laugh, fear cannot dominate. It might be a co-pilot, but not the chief in charge. This is an important and lifesaving change.

If we are unable to laugh at our troubles, it often means there is still too much hurt. We have not yet come to the place of accommodating or carrying our troubles in some contained way.

There is also mean-spirited humor, and it can be used to harm. We have to be careful of humor that is used to ignore or discount someone's life or truth without giving rise to another equal truth. The best laugh is from being shown some nugget of truth more clearly. The worst humor comes from the dishonesty of hiding hatred under the cloak of laughter, belittling those without power. A mean humor says it's OK to disrespect or even hate some folks and doesn't serve anyone's healing.

*Honesty*

Honesty is also vital in making space for choice. In times of crisis, there is a tendency to say and do what looks helpful, soothing, and smoothing, even if it's not quite true. In part we do this out of love and the wish to banish pain as soon as possible. Few people are able to be around pain without trying to make it disappear or take it on. Our impatience with pain can cause us to be less clear or frank. The urgency can bring us to a place of promising things we don't know about, offering to do things we don't have time, energy, or skills to accomplish.

This impatience with pain causes people to be confused or dishonest about the most difficult aspects of their hurt or their recovery. So even when we are conscious of covering over the truth of our pain, we can signal a silent agreement with others that we won't go there, that acknowledging our pain is taboo. This might lessen pain for a time, but it can become a pattern of avoidance that takes us away from the necessary work of healing—from seeing what is and what's next. Opening ourselves to more honesty is sort of like going barefoot for the first time in years. It can feel like too much coming through too tender a place. It can also make you feel unexpectedly alive and free.

To be honest in times of crisis is to be as clear and concise as possible about what we see and know. It sets a tone that invites others to do the same. This helps everyone gather more ideas and perceptions at a time when awareness and honest assessment are most important. It can also sweep away a pattern of niceness to make way for acts of goodness. This counteracts the numbness that contraction induces and starts to awaken us to our own feelings. We don't want to feel everything all the time, but we need a wider range of choice in what we are ready for. This range is always expanding and contracting.

Honesty is valued and expressed differently in different cultures. Practices vary from country to country and household to household. What the culture says we may be honest about also varies and changes over time. What we could not discuss politely a decade ago is common dinner conversation now. Hopefully, the more we are able to say about what we feel and what we understand our condition to be, the more we will be able to see and name what's needed next.

Secrecy is an enemy of honesty and not uncommon in trauma. Many hurts happen in secret. Many hurts are carried secretly. A pattern of secret-keeping can begin with early hurt and not be obvious or conscious. One can become secretive about a corner or aspect of life without noticing. Sometimes secrecy is inherited, a family pattern. What some call discretion may be secrecy that results in dishonesty. Secrecy is contrary to all the good that can come from honesty. It's a barrier to being aware and being able to name our condition. It can become an invisible wall that feels solid without our knowing why it's a boundary.

There are, of course, many reasons not to be honest, some of them quite good. In many places and situations honesty will be unwelcome. So we must choose carefully, knowing that still waters are not very good for washing out lots of dirt.

In healing from trauma, honesty is most useful in helping us get in touch with passion, keeping in mind that hope is a passion. Honesty opens the window, allowing all deep feelings a breath of fresh air. This stirs up some truth and lessens numbness. What we love, hate, fear, need—are all aspects of our passions, our strong deep feelings. Honesty helps us get through layers of old stuff that is covering up passion, allowing us to contact hope. Connecting to hope is the first step to healing. All the passions live in the same neighborhood. If we cannot contact hope directly, it may be that if we can connect with deep feelings, hope will join the parade by and by. Feelings of anger and love live near hope and can rouse one another out of sleep and numbness.

## Compassion

Compassion is the third part of making space for choice. It is the most surgical of the tools we have to get past the rigidity of tightly crafted contraction. Our ability to love ourselves, someone else, or to receive love will make a world of difference in creating space within a compacted self. A tender look that says, "I see your hurt, and you are not alone" can reduce despair faster than anything else.

So, important questions come forward about compassion. What do we know about receiving and giving love and care in times of hurt? What do we see, regarding our love, in ourselves or others, when we are afraid? What happens to our gift of love when we can't see it being received and appreciated? What was the nature of compassion when it saved you from despair before? All that we can discover about these things will contribute to our best giving and our best receiving in the war zones of fear and anger.

In my work, I have found the following to be true of compassion: No love is ever wasted. All compassion that is expressed works to the good. It goes where it's needed though we may not be able to see this.

It's not the quantity of performance of love that saves lives from feeling lost. It's the depth of feeling, the ability to *be with* another, often not doing anything, that can be the best gift.

Healing from trauma often has the feeling of a dual movement. The wall of separation is dismantled brick by brick at the same time a new platform for a wider—and truer—view is being built brick by brick. Compassion is the muscle that does both works.

# Three Friends

When we set out to do some work, we choose our tools carefully, maybe we have some idea of what might be involved, and perhaps we even know how long it might take. These bits of information help us to maintain a certain attitude and momentum for taking on everything from cleaning the bathroom to working for justice.

In the long-term task of healing trauma or helping someone else to heal, there are three friends who do a tight little dance that will either propel us forward to do our best or add to the pain and confusion. So we must keep careful track of these friends and see if we're setting up to do our best for the long haul. These three friends are intention, confidence, and trust.

## Intention

The first friend is intention. What is needed, what is it we hope to get done, what do we think we are capable of? All of our experience, history, and knowledge are brought to bear in creating an intention. If the task is to get from the staircase to the piano without touching the floor, it's our job to remember or imagine whether such a thing is possible for us or possible at all. Have we done such a thing before? Have we done anything remotely similar so we can transfer the wisdom from a related experience?

Then we want to consider our particular gifts. Each of us has characteristics or talents that make us well-suited or ill-suited for certain tasks. Does the work in front of you now suit your gifts in some ways and not in others?

Finally, we want to take a look at our gut level response to doing this work. In your heart of hearts, how do you feel about carrying out this task or series of tasks? And perhaps most important, how will that feeling affect doing the task tomorrow and later on? Carefully considering what we know and feel about the work that confronts us will help us do our best work. A well-chosen intention makes our work better and easier to do.

## Confidence

The second friend is confidence. Confidence is a beautiful thing. In crisis it is positively essential. One large firm rock to cling to is not much reason for joy in the middle of a hay field on a lovely summer's day, but in a stormy sea it can mean life.

Confidence needs to be as solid as its appearance. It's not confidence that claims the gas tank is full without checking and leaves the riders stranded down the road. Confidence is a feeling of wholeness that is based upon realistic assessment of known facts and a hopeful outlook, a combination of what we know and how we approach the mess we're in. Knowledge alone does not fend off fear or calm hysteria. And a positive outlook must be supported by good information. This is not to say we should never travel with less than a full knowledge of a well-planned trip; much of what we need we acquire on the road. But we want to have as much information as possible to support our confident attitude when we begin our trip.

Can we feel reasonably sure that good things will come out of our efforts? Do we have a sense that we can probably do the work in front of us? Can we know the outcome is not in our control and still give our best with a clear vision of what might be possible? Can we agree to the parts we have skills, know-ledge, and experience in? Can we acknowledge the parts we have no clue for? Do we know where to look for help along the way? What steps can we take to help us feel more secure?

*Trust*

Trust is the place of the broadest perspective. From the standpoint of trusting ourselves and what the future holds, we can see what we understand and what we haven't a clue about, what we enjoy and what we cannot tolerate, what we expect to turn out as we hoped and what is going to be hell on wheels. Trust at its essence is a meeting of what we know and how we feel, resulting in a sense that we are being clear and in some way OK. The mind and the heart concur on their individual assessments of someone or some situation where good work seems possible. The reliability of both perceptions agreeing is a comfort. This sets the stage for openness even in the midst of hard choices and difficult tasks, honesty with ourselves. The capacity to trust, ourselves or others, is an accumulated wisdom reflecting our experience. It has a center and won't be easily moved about by the various noises of today, but the edges move to show how comfortable we are in the immediate environment.

~

Here is how the three friends dance. When we choose an intention either deliberately or unconsciously, we set a course which affects our confidence and our trust. If we choose well confidence and trust increase. If we choose poorly, the spiral is downward.

Let's say I witnessed a scene of incredible pain and choose to respond immediately. Let's say I saw the AIDS epidemic and wanted to help make it less painful, and out of my love I volunteered right away, but out of my fear and revulsion to pain I promised too much. This resulted in exhaustion fairly soon after beginning. The exhaustion decreased my confidence because I could see no end in sight and my own personal resources were quickly dwindling. As I lost confidence in doing the tasks before me, my capacity to trust myself and gain others' trust would diminish also. The spiral would be downward.

Now what if I came upon a scene of great pain and considered what needed doing and what parts I had some talent for or knowledge of—and of those parts, what did I have time for? This would be choosing an intention deliberately. Then my confidence would have a chance to increase because I would have a better idea of what I was in for and the possibility for success would be larger. This would enhance my trust and my trustworthiness. The spiral would be upward. By keeping my intention more broad and less specific, I could increase my effectiveness, be flexible with change, and enjoy the work.

When we are setting out on a piece of work, the time we take to consider what maps we have and what maps we are missing will help us to choose well from the start and support our progress along the path miles after we have begun.

Keep these three friends in mind and watch to see if they are dancing together in ways to help you do your best for the long haul.

Healing Trauma

# Giving, Exhaustion, and Despair

There are some common analogies for the feeling of burnout: the well-known grouch who is awful to be around; the enormous fatigue that never seems to end no matter how much sleep we get. But for many people the combination of exhaustion and despair that constitutes burnout is more like a bottomless pit. And we are surprised that it's grown so deep and taken over so much of our life. It's as though we have been walking along a cliff, and then one day we look up to find out we fell off some time ago.

Burnout is the exhaustion of the inner self at all levels. The body, thoughts, emotions, and the essence are weary. At its worst, we experience burnout as a bottomless pit, endless fatigue, horrible grouchiness, and loss of joy, wisdom, and intelligence.

Burnout at its beginning is simply this—the desire to stay in bed or go to the beach instead of doing the work, whatever work one has committed to do. This means most of us are probably somewhere in the middle and trying to figure out our next best move.

The first obvious signs of becoming overwhelmed tend to be physical. There may be a change in the rhythms of the body. Normal patterns of sleep can transform into something not so restful, such as increased difficulty getting to sleep or waking up, frequent waking through the night, distressing dream cycles, or often feeling tired upon waking.

There might be changes in the type and quantity of the foods we are drawn to. Our appetites may get stuck in comfort foods while our digestion may reflect a constant tension, changing our normal patterns of elimination.

There also tend to be changes in patterns of emotion, perhaps settling on anger and sadness in a big way, and passing over other feelings, more fun feelings. It's not uncommon to have the small bothersome things that we had tolerated easily, suddenly become the target of great rage. And rage, unlike anger, tends not to have a healthy closure following expression. Rather, it hangs on as a constant feeling, ready to attach itself to the next annoyance. To those observing us, it's shocking.

The sadness of burnout is sneaky. It comes into the senses and is felt over and over until it seems to be the primary reality. It does not offer the relief that follows the expression of healthy sadness. It can become a shell that we feel around our hearts, covering our thoughts, and reflected in our posture and physical energy. We can be reduced into living in this mode to the obstruction of other feelings. We can feel we don't have enough energy to experience joy or that we don't have room for it. So, our fatigue, and perhaps an unconscious decision, may keep us on a path of deadened enjoyable feelings and captive to non-enjoyable feelings.

There can be a loss of intellectual balance and perhaps even some paranoia. Wisdom is diminished. Response tends to be oversized and either premature or terribly late. The combination of emotional fatigue and loss of judgment has made history in the worst ways. Some of the most dreadful politics to be witnessed are in our non-profit crisis organizations where good, hard working people have mistaken each other as the enemy. I have seen some grand tragic opera take place and devour wonderful people doing great work because the feelings of despair became a "good guys vs. bad guys" mind set. The real enemy in burnout is not people but rather weariness, defensiveness, and the refusal to learn. When we are in pain and confusion, learning can be too much to ask. Yet it is often the solution combined with rest to restore balance to the intellect.

Giving itself is not well understood in our culture. Giving of oneself to others during their times of pain and confusion has potential for serious mistakes. Much of this giving is relegated either to immediate relations or professionals. Depending on one's experience and training, this can often bring people to give inappropriately. Giving inappropriately is the primary cause of burnout. The secondary cause being that work is not acknowledged to be as difficult as it is.

There are two myths in particular from our culture that set people up for inappropriate giving resulting in burnout. They are both so intrinsic to how we live that they are unseen. We might know the gross aspects of one myth and yet be unaware of how some lesser part of it modifies our response in crisis.

*The Gunslinger*

One cultural myth is exemplified by the role of the lone gunslinger hero in the many U. S. western and war movies. There is an essential message that goes, "If we all get together right now and push, we can change this. If we shove hard enough, all that is broken can be fixed and all that is ugly can be made beautiful. We can handle this through tough hard quick action. Then it will be over and we can go home." This is usually led by a singular hero.

In reality, there is no crisis that can be taken care of quickly, easily, and only through toughness. It's great entertainment and fantasy relief but skews the picture of our lives. Healing deep hurt requires much time, hard work, and a good deal of tenderness. What can be done quickly is only preliminary. Toughness might be an aspect of the courage needed, but without aspects of surrender there will be no receiving and therefore no learning or resolution.

On the one hand we want to push hard now and get it done out of our love so that no one is left in pain. But it is also true that very few of us can bear to be around pain. It's a kind of slumming that unnerves us to witness the fragility of life. So we push not only out of our love, but also from our not wanting to be near suffering.

The lone gunslinger hero myth brings people to work with an idea in the back of their minds that large positive change can be made now. It equates effort and single-mindedness with the ability to conquer. This may be suitable for getting out of the burning house, but not for the treatment of burns, grieving losses, or liberating the body and mind from the recurring memory of the flames. The result is often that we get a short way into the work of dealing with trauma and get impatient or discouraged that the crisis has not diminished quickly or easily. We feel a sinking feeling after a time that we are tired from the work yet there doesn't seem to be any less work to do. On the contrary the monster may seem the same or larger, while we feel smaller. We are not only wounded, but we are also going uphill, limping, wondering why we didn't know the hill would be so steep and long. The myth of quick and tough gives us the wrong pace for doing a long piece of work.

Once we feel our personal resources decrease in the face of all the work, our tone changes. We often try to work harder and faster. We begin to blame ourselves for not doing and being enough. Often we begin to blame those around us for not doing enough. Here's where the politics of getting well start to seem like cat fights in the alley. Being afraid that despite our best efforts things are not getting better is destructive to our sense of intention and motivation. Especially when getting well has been assumed quietly all along. The work is now a landslide, and we are too hurt, tired, and overwhelmed to manufacture more fits of optimism. When this happens, folks start wondering if they should give up. And though it may seem a bad choice on a short menu, people often do give up for a time, sometimes for good, adding a sense of failure to frustration and fatigue.

There is a second cultural myth that brings people to inappropriate giving, exemplified by the heroines in love stories who suffer greatly for the love of a good man. In this myth, the one who gives until she has nothing left is the winner. But the win may not include the love or the man or getting back what she's lost. It might be only that she is gazed upon admiringly by others as someone who gave her all, even to her own destruction. The subtle cultural message here is directed largely to women, but also to caregivers in general. The message is this: "Look at how good she is. She gave until there was nothing left." And "If you give until you are empty, your goodness will be confirmed by others. If you exhaust yourself, they will throw a parade for you, and you shall be declared Queen of the May." This myth is deep within our culture. The desire to have others confirm our goodness for acts of selflessness grows like weeds. It's a trap for every person who might be good at giving, has a gift for compassionate response, or has had little experience of learning personal power, self-esteem, or especially, a sense of their own goodness.

This myth is dangerous because it promises something that will never come. If you completely exhaust yourself in the service of your own or someone else's healing, you will be unable to continue where there is great need. Rather than a parade, the more likely response to this situation is someone else is brought in who can keep things going. There may be a thank-you gift, and maybe some pity, but no parades, unless being carried out on a stretcher counts.

The important lesson here is that we do not need to have our goodness confirmed. *We are already good.* We began that way, and we remain good. Imperfections are only that, details to be worked on along the way. They are not reason enough to give oneself over to ruin for an untrue promise of hoorays. Our goodness is now and real. It can be experienced every day through feelings of love and gratitude. We do not honor anyone by exhausting ourselves into further suffering. We help no one by giving too much or hurting ourselves. No one is served by our joining their suffering.

This myth brings many people to burnout each day. It includes the inability to say no and does not separate the experience of the giver from the receiver. Even when we give to ourselves, there is the need to feel and know both roles evenly. To give without focus or boundary is a sign of a needy, shallow compassion that spreads too thin too soon.

The overall feeling as this part of one's personal opera comes to its climax is betrayal. After giving all there is to give, instead of rewards there is only greater need on all parts and little clarity as to what happened. On stage it can make for great music. In life it can be too hard to bear for its lessons escape us.

There is a great need to understand the place of giving in our lives, especially when it is done in the context of trauma where giving is surrounded by intimacy and urgency.

Let me use the analogy of an apple tree. You have a beautiful apple tree and you decide to give away all your apples every year. Wonderful. So you make sure that tree is in a place where it's going to get sun and rain because it needs both. You take care to be sure that no small animals are living in the roots. Maybe you have a fence around the tree so that deer are not eating the apples. You prune back the sucker branches of this tree in late winter or early spring. By and by comes harvest when the apples are large and juicy, weighing down the limbs with the beautiful fruit. You take them all down and give them all away. Wonderful.

Now let's say someone comes to me the next year in mid-summer, weeping and begging for me to give them some of my apples. They are truly in need and I have committed myself to giving them all away. But when I look to my tree, the apples are not ready yet. They are not the right color or size. They wouldn't taste very good. They would not be nutritious and thus not a very good gift. And where the apple is taken from the tree too early, the tree will not bear there again.

~

The first thing to be remembered about giving is that it begins and depends on having a strong sense of self. By having a strong sense of self and caring for our inner resources, we have more to offer for a longer time. Personal love is a finite, renewable resource. It must be refreshed carefully each day for sufficient renewal to give more away. Each of us only has so much to give away each day. That measure of love can grow and the muscle for it can become strong. But it will always require the balance of receiving to be restored to do more. Divine love is infinite and any number of things might happen that seem impossible when divine love is involved. But most of us roll up our sleeves each day using our personal love to do our work, so great care must be taken for that love to be kept bright and burning.

We must have a reverence for our giving, a great care and feeling of importance for the loving we have to offer to places of hurt for ourselves or others. Knowing that what we give is not just some little nothing we cast off with no effect, but that each giving has value and meaning to be recognized before, during, and after delivery.

Kindness is an act of reverence for all of humanity. Kindness shines Light to help us all see the true nature of life. By bringing reverence to our giving, we remove it from the plain handing over that is barely distinguishable from getting rid of something. We bring it into the place of importance where the tone of love clears and cleans the areas that this giving touches. Gone is the promise of cheering crowds replaced with the calm quiet of knowing you are part of a larger design than you can fathom.

Recovery from burnout is a very particular work as difficult as any healing. Once we have become exhausted, overcome with despair and terminally grouchy, then comes the task of restoration of all that is weary. This takes two outrageous luxuries—time and patience. Time is a quality so valuable that even some very wealthy people don't have it. It is the luxury of time that will provide the renewal and perspective of returning to balance. Patience is required because this recovery is a long internal combination of rest and seeking. It calls for changing some external details, but largely the work will be on the inside, some of which will be hard to see. So patience is essential.

The first task is to check our balance of giving and receiving. Where do we do our giving, what is the nature of it, the tone, what becomes of that giving, and how did we come to give this and whom does it affect? What history and baggage are connected to it?

Then let's take an equally deep look at where we have our receiving, where do the hugs and kisses come from, who sees us and knows us warts and all, what brings comfort, where does it come from, what and whom do we depend on and with what measure of joy? In the various roles you have in your life today how many of them are primarily as a provider and how many of them are as receiver? Is our giving and receiving in balance, or are they disproportionate in one direction or the other? Then we set about redoing that balance. It will mean saying no and choosing

Healing Trauma

who and what is important and speaking that truth. This is graduate school you cannot drop out of.

Here's something that scares many people, but I find to be very true and helpful in putting into perspective the importance of good care for ourselves. If you completely exhaust yourself by giving work, it will only take you twice as long to recover as it did to become tired, and only if you are very careful in your self-care.

Did you hear that? Twice as long to get well from burnout as it took you to burn out—if you're careful. So, let's attend to the level of fatigue and despair we have now before the homework and timeframe increases.

There is every reason to learn these lessons. There's nothing here that is impossible. Let's go forward bit by bit, use what we know, learn some, and make the changes we need. There is much good that needs doing and much learning to enjoy in doing it.

# Living Through Grace, Living on Gifts

When I was thirty years old I resigned from my job as a preschool teacher. Salary, retirement, paid vacations, savings account, health insurance, sick leave—all hung up like an old worn coat. I stepped out, out into what appeared to be thin air. I needed something more than the usual. What I had thought would be a move to a more interesting way of making a living became a practice of faith and hope.

Imagine that you had a particular passion that made you different in the way you considered parts of life. Not so unusual really. Now picture using that passion to focus and hone your abilities in a way that insists on improving yourself, your surroundings, and the lives you come in contact with. Still not so out of the ordinary. Now bring in an element of being paid—not necessarily by the people you serve, but by people who see and understand that your work is important. And instead of being paid per task, you are paid as people are moved. This is the thin air part. Not because there is nothing there, but because the culture teaches us that there is not enough.

When we bring the essence of our best understanding and effort forward, our measure of the Inner Light glows brighter and longer. We come to know a center of who we are, Divine connection, our individual worth and the possible value of corporate effort. What we know and what we are still learning becomes clearer. What fills us with excitement and what bores us to tears becomes amazingly real.

What are the cultural systems and traditions that encourage this dynamic, this simple ideal of how to be in the world? And what cultural traditions drag down this spirit of knowing the self?

Money is itself one of those topics such as evil, sex, or violence, that is so private and pervasive we are never certain if we have received a proper education about them or what a proper education might look like. So let's sidestep as much cultural baggage as possible and say that money is a vehicle for offering more choice. And like anything that has power, it must be used carefully.

People have always supported good works in many ways, and I have entered that tradition. When I receive a gift of money, I know that it's because someone has recognized my riches and understands that I am sharing them. It's a way of joining me and giving a push to a work they want to see continue. If people gave

Healing Trauma

me money because I was poor, I would only experience myself as I was seen, as only needy. My sense of myself begins with my connection to the Divine. The messages, the opportunities, the strength are all blessings that come forward, invited and not. My primary task is surrender, surrender of disbelief including fear and doubt. The listening to what is being asked of me for my own healing as well as others follows this immediately. Surrender and listening over and over, then sometimes action is the overall pattern. Some of what is presented is to inform me of what I cannot help, an abiding humility to tether my reckless heart.

My gift for releasing pain is inconstant. I do not choose when or to whom the gift is given. The faith to say yes and the faith to say no are the same on the inside. One hopes that it can be seen and understood on the outside. My dedication to the work is *not* inconstant, and my ability to be ready increases with each year of practice.

There is a small dance that is done to balance two forces. On the one hand, the work, in my understanding, is intimate and needs to be kept low to the ground. Intimate work is easily misunderstood or misinterpreted the larger the group one works with. So there is some need to be able to watch and see if each one participating in healing work is engaging similar understandings and experience of unfolding. On the other hand, there is some need for enough people to see the work and appreciate its importance to support the work prayerfully and financially. I think of this dance as not pushing the river, while watching for currents of clarity and kindness that will carry us farther along.

There are lots of ways to get off the path and generally one way to get back on—go back to basics. Follow your disciplines and do good work. Support will change as the work does and as we grow with the work. As we learn to be graceful in our own dance between hope and fear, our support from others will reflect that grace.

# Section 6

## From the Journals

Afterwards                          145

Cambodian Grandmothers              147

Comadres                            149

Lubicon Lake Nation                 153

The OK Boy                          155

Hattie                              156

The Phone Rings                     160

The Saddest One                     162

# Afterwards

I lay my hands on an old friend who lies very still and weary, her breath small and her color slightly gray. She is tired from a long life fully lived and battles with illness that have not been won. I hold her feet, slide hands under her hips, and slowly rock with hands under one scapula and one thigh. As she slides into sleep and a cute little snore, I wonder "When is it OK to go?" When has life been enough, long enough, that it's OK to leave it and die?

Do I wonder this because she's getting ready? I'm not sure. Do I wonder this because I have a birthday next week that brings me within three years of sixty? Maybe. Do I wonder this because I feel the weariness in her that I've felt in so many who eventually nod and say *"Yes, time to go, it's been enough."*

I know that pain and suffering can bring one to longing for an end. But I wonder if for most it's not more subtle than this—could it be that one can just no longer see how beautiful that day is, or how wonderful it is that spring has come again, or feel revived by the look of love in another's eyes? Mostly I sense that people leave when life is just too much to be here any longer. I wonder about that too-much-ness. Maybe that's just what I'm seeing on the outside.

What is it like on the inside to feel that shift that it's time to go? Is it beyond decision, something we just sense the way dogs seem to when they go off to die? Is it a spiritual shift? Is it like delivering a child whose schedule is different from the mother's?

When this old friend finally goes I can imagine the most subtle changes taking place. Will she float above herself and marvel at the sensation of being free of that old wreck of a body? Will she wonder to see the grief that will surround her former body? Will she wonder at the love she feels? What is the scheduling like after this? Surely there must be some kind of welcome or instruction or explanation to that other side. I've heard from several elders of others coming to help them cross over.

After a few hugs and kisses of old dears, is there a slide show of choices? The offer to have a shower and a nap after such an arduous crossing? A foot bath perhaps? Is there reassignment straight away? Some catching up about what that last eighty years meant down there in all that human confusion? Does the concept of time cease to be? Is essence kept and body gone as an identity?

What are the choices to send word back that all is well and hell is only what they are doing to one another back there in *reality*?

By and by as her sleep deepens, I remove my hands and quietly scoot out the door to let her sleep. I want to make her be at home and rest more, but that is my own selfishness, wanting her to stay here longer. Her daughter says, "Yes she's doing too much."

Stay with us a while longer, old friend. See how beautiful the day is? See how bright the spring flowers? How lush the summer will be and how sweet the corn. So many of us love you. Stay. My private request spoken only inwardly is just one small part of the many pieces in her consideration and timing the time to go.

# Cambodian Grandmothers

*1993*

On this quiet morning I am at my desk as a bit of snow and sun mix in the sky. It's beautiful. The woodstove is on a slow burn, but the rest of the woodpile is refusing to get into the woodshed by itself. I have been going back over my 1993 calendar as I answer some letters, months overdue. There are flashes of memories of stories, people, teaching, and travel. This year I worked with twenty-seven different groups in three countries. Though much of it seems a blur now as I begin a resting time, certain stories and images are strong, especially from the last trips.

I spent a Sunday in October as the guest of my friend Malis. She's a social worker near Boston helping Cambodian refugees settle in the U.S. We met in 1988 at an international conference on torture in Costa Rica. She brought me in to do work at her house a few years before. She would come in with a few people, tell me the gist of their experience, and while I worked with them, she'd fetch a few more and give me a brief history, "This women saw all her children murdered. This child lived alone in the jungles eating whatever she could find until she found the border and then was raped by guards at the camps. This man was left for dead after his torture. This woman lost all the men in her family."

This time she arranged to have a dozen refugees meet with me at the home of a Buddhist priest, all are Cambodian grandmothers tortured by the Khmer Rouge

In a large empty room with a mat on the floor, each woman in turn lies down and rests while I say my prayers for guidance asking where my hands should go. I sit holding feet or shoulders or head or other places where ache and soreness held the memories of earlier hurt. Sometimes I feel the sadness or physical pain seep out, smooth and clear. Usually I feel the peacefulness and deep relaxation wash in like a tide of light. In the adjoining room the women wait and watch through the doorway. At first there is the utmost reverence and quiet. They each enter with hands clasped in prayer, bowing. As the day goes on, the quiet turns into talk of families and children, trying on clothes brought from home, lunch, talking about how it felt to be touched by me.

There are two women I couldn't help, but I am of use to the rest. I will never forget the look of one of the oldest women—tiny, brown, and very graceful. She entered with a combination of regal humility and sweetness. She was grateful upon rising after the work and bowed solemnly with hands together, a gesture I returned. Afterward, when she stepped to the doorway with the eyes of her peers on her, she did a little dance with raised hands, not unlike Magic Johnson after scoring the winning point.

What's most obvious to me, and what I must keep before me, is that reverence is the necessity for balancing and grounding amidst such pain. It beckons grace and hope. My primary experience of these times is one of grace and hope, the realization that all pain is essentially the same, and comfort can be given no matter what has happened. It tires me, but this fall the fatigue was in balance with the gratitude.

# Comadres

*1988*

In May, I went to downtown Washington, D.C., to a church basement and began doing work with women who had been tortured in prisons of El Salvador. They are founders of the committee Comadres, mothers and wives of the disappeared during the US-sponsored civil war there.

This is when I would like my life to be a movie so I could look at all the scenes slowly. So much goes on. I make my way through the 95-degree heat and humidity. I empty a fistful of nickels and dimes into the Metro machine to get a $1.70 round-trip ticket, my overhead for today's work.

This day I will work with Maria. Her husband was killed trying to organize a union for workers in rural El Salvador. Maria was imprisoned and tortured while carrying her fifth child.

On arrival I am saying prayers to my angels, assessing my personal energy, and asking for their help. It sounds a bit pathetic. "I am feeling awful today—mind, body, spirit, the works. I am asking, please, that some gift be made to Maria through me. I need your grace to be of any use."

Maria and I have no common language other than hope and reverence. We use some sign language at the start of each session to share what parts of her body hurt. Clasping my hands together and putting them to the side of my head I ask her how her sleep has been. She makes a frown and says, "*poquito*," a little. I put my hands at the small of my back and raise my eyebrows as if to say, "And how is this part of you?" We do the same for other parts as our work continues over time. One week she has bad headaches, another week no sleep. Another week she has fallen and bruised a knee and shoulder badly. One week she is frantic with the news that she has not been granted amnesty.

Just as in the AIDS epidemic, one must always love without attachment to the idea of controlling the larger picture. Dying, deportation, losing the one you've been helping can feel as though your work doesn't count. But that is not so. If your work is good when you are doing it, then its total remains. This is loving for the sake of loving, tough and tender at the same time, and there is always the remembering that no love is ever wasted. During that session I saw Jesus come to us in bright, electric colors and guide the work. She and I were both stunned by this. His compassion was as exquisite as Light itself.

Maria's little boy, Oscar, was in utero when much of the torture took place. Now he refuses to be out of her arms when men are present. It has meant at times that I am doing massage and energy work on Maria while she holds him. He is soon asleep in her arms as she dozes too.

There are times when she is more scared than others, and I feel myself being drained of all energy, especially if I am not well rested. There are days when we are both centered, and the silence and stillness become thick and glowing. Those times we both leave in a state of grace.

One day, I notice several things at once. She is tense as her deportation hearing approaches. Recent news of the death squads back home is terrifying and leaves her sleepless. The army has stolen supplies sent to earthquake victims and has arrested Comadres staff. I feel too tired to fend off her despair. I feel her sadness seep down into me and deplete my reserves. She will need work on the left side of her head where tension has collected. I will have to reach very deep into my own calm to do her any good. I will need to sleep after this. I will have to choose between clients and deskwork this week. I ask for her angels and mine to surround us and make her a gift of peace.

After some opening work to join intimate energies, I begin at her feet. It seems at times that the deeper the hurt, the more stillness is required to contact it. By all appearances, I am sitting on the floor, holding one foot at a time almost without motion. But the transaction I feel taking place (and not by any decision on my part) is drawing the energy and attention of her body down to her feet and opening the bottom of her feet like a trap door, releasing what feels like overcrowding. She is sitting with her eyes closed. When I ask her to lie down on the sofa, I begin to wave and weave my arms in circles to clear the area over her, a method I often use, but this motion is too coarse for how she feels today. She is more fragile, and I just sort of pat and smooth the air rather than scoop it. I feel my own tenderness rise and feel her sadness release in bits. Her sadness seeps out and I wonder if she will weep. She lies still, her face placid, and then she turns to the side just a bit. I work on her shoulders and back. My hands are on her hips and legs and follow down to her feet again.

There is a clear sense of completion and a deep grace in us both by the hour's end. Even the room feels clearer. As she rises, she looks as though she's had a good sleep. After a while she says something in Spanish, which I understand by intuition and from many other receivers. "I wasn't in my body. I was floating." The color is back in her face. Her posture is better. She is calmer and has more energy. She looks younger. We hold each other's hands and say goodbye.

There are no words for this intimacy, to feel the sadness that seeps out from the limbs and into my hands, passing through my soul and out. For a moment I feel the sadness, terror, or pain grow and then pass. No words for the look on her face as peace sneaks in like night. No words for the moment when I wonder what to do next, where to touch, what happened here two years ago. Will a touch there scare her? Will it hurt? Will it release a flood of sadness that will overwhelm us both? Will I lose my center and become exhausted? Will I lose track of my gift, my goodness? Usually a deep breath comes, a narrow passage broadens, tension melts, and all and each of these happen several times in an hour's work.

I feel more confident in this work as the months and years go on. The stories of torture have frightened me. I don't repeat the stories because it feels like flirting with insanity or tempting evil. I have been afraid of the transfer I have experienced with other traumas. It is common for me to feel the pain of others as I work. There is a moment when the essence of a feeling rises in them and moves into me, and then out. Suddenly, we are both cleaner and they carry less around. It is not gone so much as it is less immediate, has less bite. It took me years to accept this transaction, to surrender to the experience and allow it to stretch me. I have put a great deal of effort into surrendering and making no effort to control or guide the process. I am fairly at home with it now, although it leaves me fairly tender and certainly not in a state to be downtown soon afterward, which is where I am doing this refugee work.

Later in the day I feel a deep tiredness. I recall the beginning of work with AIDS. There was always the mix of excitement, gratitude, and lots of exhaustion until I learned what my gifts were, how to govern my giving, and how to become more disciplined about my rest.

After this work, I walk the two blocks to the Metro station past several homeless men in rags sitting on the sidewalk. I get teary. It's hard to wake up a cranky grouch, feeling only my own orneriness, and then enter into grace on behalf of someone surviving the most horrendous traumas. It feels as though the sadness and hardness of my life are only a cloak that I draw over me. This work—this handing myself over to divine work—takes these extraneous details away, and I am again firmly on the earth. I walk with a lightness and a brighter vision of what's going on, what's available, what's possible.

It's sad to lose this awareness and broad perspective of life, to be in awe of its miracle, like losing one's sobriety. It's too great a contrast to move from the numbness of the modern urban rush to feeling deeply what is sacred and what has been defiled. It's too strong a reminder of what I know but lose track of too easily. How luscious the balance and stillness of grace is and how easily my own illusions and the noise of the world distract me.

# Lubicon Lake Nation

*April 1995*

Roseanna was drying moose meat on a high wooden rack over a low fire. She used a very sharp hunting knife to turn large chunks of the dark red meat into long thin ribbons, turning the blade again and again like a sculptor not wanting to cut through to the outside. A friend had shot two moose on his way to visit his parents out in the bush and had shared the bounty. The bush might be called the woods. But here in northern Alberta the land is muskeg, a boggy plain where thin trees grow densely and for many square miles the only clearings are the open water of streams and lakes or where someone brought in a large machine to change the land.

Those *someones* came after natural gas and oil reserves were located on land where the Lubicon Cree have lived for thousands of years and before the Lubicon Lake Nation concluded a land treaty with the Canadian government.

I get to know only a handful of people in my four days with the Lubicon at the end of April. Mostly, I have time with the children. A dozen or so children come to play in a social worker's living room each afternoon after school. The first three to arrive are five-year-old twins and a three-year-old who curses like a sailor at the least provocation. Elaine has bushels of Legos, which they play with every day. The others come soon afterwards and, as Elaine works on the computer in the adjoining office, I am watching the first generation of Lubicon Cree who do not have Cree as their first language. Some grandparents cannot speak with their grandchildren now for the lack of a common language.

The week before I arrived, a five-year-old boy was attacked by one of the numerous dogs in the community. He had wounds along one leg, foot to hip. He doesn't talk about the attack except to look at the floor and slowly shake his head and say quietly, "The dogs, the dogs." He spends much of the afternoon beside me cozied up under one arm. As I watch him work a small plastic puzzle, I am doing energy work on him with all my heart. What pours off of him is all of the too-much. He and his generation are the buffer zone and interface between a First Nations people on the brink of cultural destruction and the encroaching Anglo culture. The scarcity of food, the absence of potable water, even the different sense of time kept at his home and his school makes him a foreigner in two places. As the tension falls away from this little body, he sinks into the old couch more present to the intrigue of the puzzle and the comfort of being held.

A girl of about nine sits near me. She wants to know about the new things I have brought for them to play with. "And you brought all these stickers, and the pens, and the puzzles for us?" Later, as she reclines near me, she throws a toy metal truck across the room nearly hitting someone's head. I place my hand gently on her ankle and begin to say, "Don't throw sharp metal things," but before I can get the words out her long thumb nail comes down on my hand like a knife poised to ward off an attack. She shoots me a look that can only be seen in the eyes of the sexually assaulted convinced that another trespass might be starting. I remove my hand and remember that this child must be touched only with my kindness and not with my hands. Elaine later shares her concern that this one has been sexually abused. With the road came the noise of machinery to scare off the game, changing the nature of food and life. With the road came alcohol and unemployment. Family violence and sexual abuse followed.

I work on a man who lost a father, a brother, and a son all in a few months. He understands the pain in his back is the grief he has not been able to release. As he lies still on Elaine's couch, I can feel the tendonitis in the right shoulder and the spasm of the psoas causing pain in the low back and inner thigh. For four years now the grief has held the tension in his body and caused a hardening that has become painful. Out of the left shoulder comes much grief as I hold it and gently rock a bit. As he feels this happening he tells of a dream he had recently of his son smiling and walking away, a sign to him that he is to release the sadness that has burdened him. He hurts less now. I have to go slow because there is very little touch in the culture as a whole, even in the healing work, and certainly as a white male who touches, I am an oddity.

# The OK Boy

*1996*

A woman came to me with her four-year-old son. He had witnessed the Oklahoma City bombing and become very aggressive in the few months since. He talked of bombs whenever he saw smoke. He comes into the room cute as a button, curious and squirrelly. I have only a few moments to make friends. I challenge him to race me rolling across the floor. He wins, big surprise. We race back. He wins again. He is beaming. I am nauseated.

I have to figure out a way to get my hands on him. "My, my," I say. "You must be very strong. Let me feel your hands." The tension and fear is there, flowing from him as he squeezes my hands. "Let me feel your feet." He stands on my open palms and I try to open up the channel so his overload of fear and anger can exit from the point called Bubbling Spring as it should normally. "Let me feel your back." There it is, the core of it: terror coming out as anger at the solar plexus. He is furious that he was made so frightened.

I vacuum as much as I can though he cannot stand still long. I can feel a new calm and change in him. I can feel my own tears rise. How blessed it is to reach very young hurt early before it becomes the convoluted emotional coping patterns of adults confused by their own interiors.

As I discuss things with his Mom he lies on his back and puts his feet in my belly. Again I am pulling the fear and anger out of him and rocking a bit. Slowly this moves into him pushing me over with his feet. I say, "Uh oh, I'm going to get pushed over," and he gives me a good push with both feet. I roll over and over and sprawl on the floor like a clown and he laughs deeply in a way his mother hadn't heard since the bombing. He is tickled to enjoy his power playfully. He changed deeply in moments. His mother and I are both a bit teary as they leave. His mom calls later and confirms what I have seen in my heart: moments of grace, gifts from above. All we need is enough quiet to listen and a lifetime of reaching.

# Hattie

I work on her every day now since she went into the hospital and came home with a diagnosis of a serious cancer. Each evening I call her house. Usually her best friend answers, and I ask if it's a good time for me to stop by, usually around eight o'clock. I walk through our field adjoining hers or follow the road back a hundred yards. I am in prayer and feeling the lushness of life of summer evenings.

She looks haggard and peaceful, tired and gracious. There is a feeling about her of Light and angels. There is not the fear of life-threatening disease, nor the fear of death. There is a sense of the fullness of life and gratitude, and a long life with much loving, a good life. I am drawn to work on her feet, head, and shoulders. This means I gently and firmly place my hands there and hold, sometimes with both hands, sometimes with one hand while the other makes a slow sweeping motion over other parts of her body. She has such a large spiritual life that her light extends far outward, and it feels as though I could work with her from across the room or down the hall.

Last night I felt some sense of the presence of Mary, the mother of Jesus, in the room with us, subtle and kind, almost imperceptible. When we began work in her home after the first hospital stay, I sensed that she had only a couple of months to live. Now, I am not sure about that sense. In some ways I trust it as an inward kind of knowing. Yet, outwardly, I am reluctant by etiquette and trustworthiness to mention this perception to others. Is it true what I sensed? Am I projecting my own fear? Who knows? I keep listening and thus far though I have doubt, I am inclined to trust my intuition.

One day she is in pain. Another day she's had no sleep. Another she is weak or feeling stronger. But the feeling around her is always one of tender surrender, almost a knowing that something larger than the experience of her body is taking place and that mystery between her body and her reality requires patience to understand and integrate.

I had worked on her in the hospital every day except when I was at the retreat with the Vermont People with AIDS Coalition. But I came home and worked on her that afternoon as soon as I had a nap. We knew nothing then. She was afraid but not nervous.

I worked on her just before surgery when all the news came out—rare ovarian soft tissue cancer, some of which could not be removed. I worked on her each day. I've also worked on her best friend and her eldest daughter. This is an opera of sudden and grand proportions.

*August 17*

I have not worked with her for four days. I just got tired and cranky and irritable. I did not call or help anyone during that time and now I feel much better. I have been overdoing the work and not resting enough. It felt oddly similar to the first days of getting tired in the AIDS work back in Boulder a dozen years ago. I didn't know how the tiredness had happened and I didn't see any way out. Then, I found the good help of an older healer.

Of course, I did see a way out this time. I didn't do any giving, and I slept and took good care of myself. A few days later, my view was different. I think the summer has asked too much of me. I think my time off has not been deep enough. I think the old anger I am working on is so large that rest as I usually know it is not possible. That is the major crux. To unearth old anger, to keep it present, and to rest amidst the fires—such learning!

*August 24*

I worked on her this evening after a few nights of no contact. She goes in for five days of chemotherapy beginning tomorrow. She seems healthy and well. She's done a final letter to loved ones. She is scared of chemo side effects but is otherwise clear for takeoff and peaceful. I love working on her.

*September 23*

Worked on her last night. I haven't done much of that lately. I told her that she should feel free to call me any time even though I was not able to come everyday. She is doing everything with chemo all wrong! She's gaining weight not losing. She's very up, not depressed, and has few other side effects. She looks and feels wonderful. Her strength is coming back. She is back in hospital today for another four days of chemo, her second round.

I am wondering about the feeling/message I had earlier of her having only two months. She is passing that soon and doing very well. Was that my stuff transferred? She said a lovely thing last night. She said that with all the people calling and caring for her that she has had a hard time letting it in, she felt a bit closed down. But with the work we did together last night, she felt her heart open up and able to receive all she is given. "Not a bad night's work," I laughed and turned my face to the ceiling calling out, "Thanks, everybody!"

*December 20*

Worked on her for an hour just now. It is a gray winter afternoon, and she has recently finished her fifth chemo treatment. She is installed in the larger family home until after Christmas. She was resting when I arrived. I spent a long time holding at her feet and then holding places at the torso, shoulder and knee, and belly. She is very tired. Her spirits are very good, and she talked about trips to Florida and Alaska when the treatments are over. I feel in her body the weariness of trespass and invasion. The cancer and the medical help all push her body beyond what is civil and decent, but the care she receives is excellent.

I work a long time. I feel the comfort she takes in this communion we share. We are easy with one another. We work together in silence with her only receiving and listening to herself, the sensations her body feels. I have full attention during the opening contact and am grateful for this opportunity for loving. I listen for guidance about where to hold. As I connect and feel my hands become warm, my awareness stays with her. I listen to my hands and to spiritual guidance, and I wonder about nothing in particular, rocking the baby to sleep mostly in the meanwhile. She is snoring deeply about halfway through the hour. Her body is very tired. But toward the end of the work she is awake, and when I finish, she wants conversation. What did I feel? What did she feel? How are her dreams at night and in the day? What is she thinking about before and after sleep? Is her room comfortable? Are there other changes that need to be made? How's the tailbone where she fell on the icy steps? How is her sleep? Is the closeness to family interrupting rest? We talk over all this and more.

She is in such good hands with such good care and has responded very well to treatment, but she is also very sick. The current goal is to coast along without the tension of worry and enjoy the convalescence. She does this very well. I am wary that though all is well just now, the other shoe could drop at any time. I try not to put this forward though I do mention that she will not know what her true energy level will be until a month or so after the last chemo appointment. I wonder at what I see and sense. I'm grateful for this chance to be loving and in awe of what I can't see.

# The Phone Rings

The phone rings. It's someone who is afraid and wants me to remind them about hope being older and stronger than fear. It's a woman whose hurt came early in life or a man who is dying young. It's a parent with a dying child or a fifty-year-old child with a dying parent.

The phone rings, and I am asked to reach across space to loosen the neck or the gut, the place where sickness first came, the place that was hit again and again, the hurt that happened in secret.

The phone rings, and it's an old friend or someone I met last year or someone who knew someone who heard of me. They are calling from their bedroom, from the emergency room, from their nightmares.

The phone rings, and I am just coming out of the shower, out of sleep, out of depression, out of laughter from the supper table conversation, out of work at my desk, my garden, my travels, my rest.

I hear the sobs and the story I understand. I hear the monotone of the one who is not sure why he called. I hear from the one I know how to help. I hear from the one no one is helping. I hear from the one I don't understand and don't feel any care for.

I hear from the one who needs just a little balance and encouragement, and the other one who needs all and more than I'll ever know.

The phone rings, and the lamp of love is aglow and the work has ease and grace.

The phone rings, and I pray for some gift of reverence to descend and save the caller from my rock-solid grouch.

The phone rings, and I remind myself to be in prayer, to listen tenderly, to ask for divine guidance while I listen, to ask while I listen with each ear, "What would you have of me, dear Spirit?"

I say to myself, "This hurt is not mine."

I say to myself, "This is only pain or mere terror or simply homework."

I say to myself, "Don't screw up."

I say, "I surrender to be a vessel of Divine love."

I say, "Thank you for this work."

I say, "Here we go again. Give me Saints and Angels Express! Super pronto! Now, please!"

The phone rings, and sometimes, with a moment of grace, I ask to be guided so that we may both receive comfort, healing, and protection.

# The Saddest One

*June 1999*

He may have been the saddest person I have ever seen. He had no space in him for even the possibility of joy, hope, or delight. No space in his back, so bent, bony, and empty of breathing. No space in his thoughts, so certain that his pains were the worst. No space in his heart: his rage was his entire real estate, his disappointment in life was complete, and it would not be disturbed.

As I sat listening to his horrendous stories of genuine pain, surrounded by his stacks and stacks of decades old newspapers and professional journals and books, I wondered, "How is it that he is constructed so completely devoid of hope? So many others have had similar hurt or worse and found a way out, a way to enjoy some part of life. How is it that this one crusty old alien has only his anger and hate to show for an entire life? It's not illogical. But it is very curious and very disturbing."

It seems there are some who never come to understand how people connect with people. Everyone has to learn the various parts of connecting—trust, love, flirtation, work, help, touch, conflict, words, pain, and so many others. Some of us choose time without contact, sometimes long periods alone. Some parts can be hard to learn and maybe never become smooth. But his particular condition of having no connections, *none*, seems so extreme.

As I touch his back, he assures me that nothing can be done, no kindness can reach all the pain he's had in his life. His clarity and certainty is rock solid. Then why did he invite me here? During the moment of quiet I feel the warmth in my hands grow. But his skin is cool and there is no comfort in his body, no place where he is comfortable within himself, never content just to be, no flat place just for resting. There are stacks of anger, fear, and loneliness. I can feel the desire for and the fear of sex churning within him. This part of his hurt came very early. It's the distrust from this hurt that has isolated him so thoroughly.

I suppose I should be glad that we don't lose more people more completely to all the hurts that life is so full of. Sometimes it hurts so much just to be alive. But many days after I leave his crowded home, his cast iron combination of despair and anger stays with me. I wonder at the how and why of his condition. Why do so many others find some Light at the end of the long difficult road and this one finds only more hurt from within?

From the Journals

Each night and morning I say my prayers for everyone who is in pain, for everyone who cannot get home, for everyone who is afraid, for everyone who is being hurt right now. I say a special prayer for all who have no soft places inward or outward to rest, to fall upon, to lay down the hurt.

# Section 7

# Home Life

21st Wedding Anniversary                                    167

A Letter to the Governor                                    169

A Rainy Evening                                             171

Adoration                                                   172

Did It Hurt to Listen?                                      173

Dinner Guests                                               176

First Fire                                                  178

My Life as a Short, Fat, Italian, Gay Quaker,
Who Can Yodel                                               179

Safe Harbor                                                 183

Slightly Murderous                                          184

The Turkey & the Saw                                        189

Thanksgiving 2001                                           190

Hospitality and Healing                                     192

Sauce and Meatballs                                         193

Making Bread                                                196

# 21st WEDDING ANNIVERSARY

*August 26, 2010*

Twenty-one years ago today, Marshall Brewer and I were married under the care of the Putney Friends Meeting in an ancient meeting house a few towns north of Putney. Almost 200 people joined us to witness our public declarations of love between two men. We each had family there and friends we'd known when we were both schoolteachers, and there were tons of queer Quakers.

Tonight we toasted with a sweet champagne, watched a movie, and tucked in early. I read Marshall to sleep and came back to work at my computer a few hours, our usual evening. Life is better and sweeter now than I ever could have dreamed of as a young person. When I think of life before Marshall, I have some sense of myself as half a soul wandering around asking various men, "Is it you?" None of them were. Not one of them was who I was searching for. Of course I didn't know who I was searching for until I found him, and then a feeling deep in my gut said—*Uh-Oh!*

I asked one of my very much older lesbian friends what it meant to feel some fear about a possible new love. She said quite honestly, "The only thing I know about relationships for sure is that when it's all over, it's their fault!"

Marshall and I had three dates and decided to spend the rest of our lives together. (I don't think this is our first life together.) Three years later we were married on a bright, beautiful summer day with fabulous food and cake. The reception line went on for hours, and if someone hadn't brought food to us, we would have starved. We still have the big blue plate that held the wedding cake.

Of course, back in 1989 a gay wedding was news, and one in a religious context was even more rare. Our wedding announcement in the local paper was the first gay wedding announcement on a wedding page in a mainstream newspaper in the United States and was read later on NPR's *All Things Considered*.

John Meyer tied Marshall's bowtie. It was a lovely silk tie with swirls of blue and champagne pink. I wore a long gauzy linen coat. I told the dress shop I wanted something like a cross between Bea Arthur and Moses. I don't know why, but this scared salespeople in three states.

Well, it's been a lovely ride. Even in my most discouraged, despairing, downtrodden bummer of moments when all hell has broken loose in my mind, and old tapes assure me that all is lost due to my completely inferior state, I can shake my fist at the sky and say, "Yeah? Well, Marshall loves me!" The longer one is in love, the fewer dark clouds loom over time. And the more one is sure and certain of love.

He can cook, too! He got two ovations for that last wedding cake he was hired to make. Two! And I've taught him a few things. He's less innocent now, although I do believe innocence is truly ingrown in Marshall. He's a true gentleman, while I am doing my best to appear as a gentleman. I have good stationery. I have belts that match my shoes. I even remember not to pee outside when we are away out in the world. But being a gentleman is really more natural with him.

It is a miracle to have one's life saved by love, but to love as much as one wants is luxury beyond words. I'm so glad I've had a really good turn at this thing—true love. It's not to be missed.

Home Life

# A Letter to the Governor

*2001*

March 1, 2001

The Honorable Howard Dean
Governor of Vermont
State Capitol Building
State Street
Montpelier, VT

Dear Howard,

The Town Report for Putney came in the mail the other day. I just wanted you to know that it lists thirty-nine civil unions registered through our town clerk, and there is no sign of locusts, famine, earthquakes, plague, cross-burnings, or dying sugar bushes. I know this has been on some people's minds for the past year. The claims of God's wrath were quite specific. I may not have a good sense of this all since I live so far south, but I do not have the impression that God is out of work or ignoring our beautiful state. I think there may simply have been some mistaken translations about God's job description.

We are doing OK down here in Putney. As you may recall, at last year's town meeting our town voted in favor, not of Civil Unions, but of gay marriage, the only Vermont town to do so, if I recall correctly. I am not disappointed with the Civil Union law. I understand that mainly people can only understand the neighbors who they have over for coffee and cake. We have lots of coffee and cake here in Putney, so mainly there is a generous idea of who our neighbors are. I think that's an idea God likes about Putney. But that's just my opinion.

Now, this new bill to equate gay couples with incest, to outlaw even the idea of gay marriage, well, I am sure you can see that this is just plain mean. My husband, Marshall Brewer, and I were married by our Quaker Meeting in Putney. We've been together fifteen years now. I've had a ministry in that church for nineteen years for people healing from trauma.

I'm sure you know all about trauma after last year's legislative session. Marshall finds graduate students for the School for International Training. He's just back from Bangladesh, where he saw SIT programs helping to empower women as leaders and wage earners. Such change increases the civil benefits for all society in that country. Those changes are coming slowly. If Vermont is not ready to give us a state marriage certificate, we understand. But please don't let them pass a law saying our life together is the same as incest. That would hurt too much. It would make us wonder whether God ever leaves Putney to shed Light in other places.

Sincerely,

John Calvi

# A Rainy Evening

*September 2012*

A rainy evening here in southeast Vermont. Just cold enough to make a fire in the wood stove, the first of the season. The fall colors are coming slowly—the yellows seem drab, maybe because we've had too little rain the last couple of months. Maybe in a few weeks when the reds come in there will be more delicious colors.

While Marshall is in the kitchen making roast pork, I stroll down to the cow pasture and give the steer corncobs and husks from last night. The pigs and sheep are envious. The neighbor gives me tomatoes, and on the way back up the little hill I dig my toes into the mud to encourage the rain runoff to go off the dirt road. I'm just back from seeing a friend who might have cancer and Marshall just off the phone recruiting English teachers for Saudi Arabia. He tells me that in the wee hours this morning he found an ancestor already established as an American in 1745.

Tomorrow we celebrate Korean Thanksgiving, *Chuseok*, with Korean friends. Marshall will cook up a storm. I am preparing for some last trips of teaching to eight groups in three states and a week-long visit from my book editor who will ask me to decide this and that and to write tons. All the self-discipline of a flash flood delays my preparations. I've been too busy to mourn the leaving of summer. Oddly, I've bought six books in the last year. All sit on my nightstand awaiting me. I try not to feel bullied. These are things I want to know but must push to get through.

I've been wondering about the phrase *walk away*. Sometimes it means to get clear of. Sometimes it means to abandon. Sometimes it means freedom. Sometimes it's learning a new discipline. I can't safely walk away from the fire I've just built. It needs tending. Marshall can't walk away from the roast for very long or it might burn. My friend cannot walk away from her cancer, if she has it. The steer refuses to walk away from the corn husks. I walked away from my family at eighteen. I walked away from "being straight" with that first boyfriend in the backseat of a Mustang at eighteen. Maybe that was the real first fire. Whole worlds open when we walk away, maybe.

Much later Marshall is sleeping. The dishwasher churns. I hear either a bat or a bird or a mouse making some space between the ceiling and the roof. Hoping this finds us all well and comfortable. Hoping we have some time to wonder and rest before we begin again.

# Adoration

*February 2009*

One of the luxuries of my marriage is still a surprise to me. It's just this: I could love Marshall as much as I wanted with no upper limit. I mean, I could be lavish and lush with my love and expressive beyond what has ever been welcomed in my life, and he would do the same. This is luxury beyond words.

How is it that loving as much as I wanted became the home I was looking for? I first noticed this in my trauma work. All the people that I worked with—rape survivors, people dying with AIDS before we even had that name, refugees—each and every person wanted some intimacy of compassion and care that could be trusted. I had to watch very carefully to see how and what might be received for care. Then in the best calm and hopefulness, a gift was made in just such a way as to be a comfort. Maybe it was the sure touch or the soft music or my constant calm in the face of their pain. But it was a work of hard and heavy love that needed just the right thing delivered in just the right way. You could do this as much as was possible as long as it was graceful.

I remember feeling this also as a teacher of young children. It was easy to feel love for them and a wonderful experience to find ways to teach that made them happy to be in school. It was the hard work again of observation and careful delivery of just the right thing at the right time. This professional love and care also felt like a huge relief, like coming home to being and doing my best self.

I suppose I had that in some friendships, too, though I don't recall close friends in early life. The boyfriends in retrospect seem to be a series of fumbling attempts at connection—between wanting to surrender and not trusting.

Really it was only with Marshall that I found that ground where one can adore another and receive this in return with the most amazing results over time.

# Did It Hurt to Listen?

*Out in the Mountains, GLBTQ newspaper of Vermont*
*March 2000*

"The State House was full of civility." The press reports said so. But that was not my experience. There were many insults. If you listened to or saw or read these insults, they probably left a stain somewhere in you. It would be hard to be called an abomination, morally sick, the downfall of civilization, unfit, and mentally ill without having some sense of insult and slander. So what did you do with those words that hurt? What's happening now that you listened to those words?

For almost twenty years, I have been helping people to get well from trauma. I've been working with tortured refugees, sexually abused women, and people with AIDS. I have some ideas for getting clean and clear from the words that go deep and hurt. I hope you find them helpful.

What we do with hurtful words is part family history, the patterns in conflict we see growing up. A child sees how insults are shaped and sees their sources and meaning. A child also sees some options for response or non-response and the consequences of choosing them. But as children, we do this learning without much conscious intent. We may learn things that do not help or are not healthy.

What we do with words that hurt also depends on whether we have a sense of our own goodness. By this, I don't mean self-esteem; that relates more to the outward idea of how we fit in. Rather, I mean the clear inner sense that at our essence we are good, and that this goodness has power. This sense of goodness accumulates from the give and take of kindness and from the rules we decide are important and should be kept. It might have a spiritual frame, or it might be modeled after the person whose light we're most drawn to.

In assessing our reaction to hurting words, we should ask ourselves, "Is there any part of this I can laugh at? Can I see any of the absurdity and laugh at it?" If we can do that it's generally a sign that we have found some way to accommodate the pain these words bring. It's as though we've made some understanding with parts of the process. This would exclude sarcasm, which is part anger and part fear. Real humor would show some sense of knowing truth about yourself and others. It could have a bite to it, but its power would be to reveal honesty more than to be used as offense.

If humor is not possible around these hurtful words, maybe the echoes of earlier hurt are very strong within us and leave no room for humor or understanding.

Then ask: "Can you remember the first times when you were oppressed?" Autobiographical memory teaches us the obstacles we faced and the moves we made because of them. Can we connect the dots between the times we were separated for difference and the ways we responded over the years? Who were our allies? Where was safe space? What did we tell ourselves about the oppressors and ourselves?

Fourth, there are some frames we can put around hurt to consider its meaning. The first frames are the personal or emotional choices made about friends and honesty. Do you remember how it felt then and know how it feels now? How does this make up some of who you are? Where was there hurt along the way? What did you do with that hurt?

The second frames are professional and political, the more obvious choices and strategies we make to keep our power in the world: income, living and work places, laws, and generally keeping worldly options open. What do you know about the choices you made (and make) for strength and dignity along the way? What has that meant in your knowledge of power and its uses?

Fifth, there is the spiritual aspect to consider. The great teachers of resistance to oppression—Gandhi, King, Buddha, Jesus, and Audre Lord, among others—understood their struggle was connected to things greater than themselves. This gave them the rare perspective not to take insults quite so personally.

They understood that light would always naturally gather some dark. They understood they were to break unjust rules and then stand there and talk about it until all hell broke loose. Hell breaking loose all around them was the first part of the reorganization, part of the reach towards something better.

Sixth, if you have the long view, the noise of insults might appear to be just so much static. However, if you are still ringing with the hurt of early oppression, there might not be much room for that bigger view. You know the person who has been openly gay since before there were clubs to join, has gone on to make a life, help others to do the same, and has the scars to show for it?

This is where that person becomes an elder in our tribe. This is not a matter of age really, but of passionate work and living and reflective attentiveness.

So let's take a moment to see how the bothersome words are painful for you and what history you have to ponder before the next step.

There are some practical ways to process all the hate surrounding us now amidst the gay marriage debate.

Talk to close friends about all you heard and how you felt. Can you remember details or general impressions? What are your feelings right now? Can you say when you've felt this way before?

Anger is important. Can you learn how to get angry, express it, and then learn how to move out of it by watching very carefully where the peak is? Can you get playful with anger, keeping in mind that it is a steppingstone, not a homestead?

What are your sources of hugs and kisses in all their varieties? Be in close touch with the loved ones you trust most, and let them know what's going on.

Watch for the usual signs of deep stress—uncomfortable changes in sleep, dream life, appetite, digestion, elimination, fear, anger, and fatigue. Give yourself all you need to relax deeply whenever possible.

Watch for the things that rest the body, bring delight and joy to the emotions, and free the mind, and put these things into regular use. Suffering is neither efficient nor attractive.

Stay very honest with all your feelings.

At the very least, I'd like to suggest we sit down with a cup of tea over by the window. Let's watch the snow fall slowly. Let's quietly go over where we've been, where we are, and know our paths. When people are trying to say who we are with insults, it's time to remind ourselves deliberately and consciously that we know what is and is not true.

# Dinner Guests

*4/25/04*

Last night and tonight, Marshall and I had guests to dinner. Marshall makes a menu and I shop for it all. I put the house in order and, while I am not so good at cleaning, I am excellent at tidying. I spend some time choosing which napkins and placemats and dishes I'll use to set the table. I take special care to light many candles and clean the kitchen so Marshall will have plenty of space to work wonders with mere groceries. As we bustle in these chores, by and by, our home is made lovely with the tasks of hospitality. The aroma of cooking, the candlelight on polished wood and old silver and crystal, the woodstove cozy and burning, and our one-big-room home becomes an embrace.

I am thinking of this tonight because of the many friends I would love to have to dinner, but who are too far away. How lovely it would be to hang up Eric's coat, to serve Elisabeth one of Marshall's special desserts, to bring Sean another glass of wine, to show Billy the new painting, to give Mark an extra helping of potatoes, to offer Louise some slippers, to ask Liz if she'd like some more chicken, to pass the basket of good crusty bread to so many others who come to mind.

Hosting brings such lovely comforts and irreplaceable luxuries. All the laughing we did the other night, hearing how Carol surprised Ry, who was in the shower, by coming in wearing only flippers, mask and snorkel, and mumbling, "Would you please soap my back?" All the joy and pride we feel to hear Suzanne talk about the three novels she is working on and the readings for the first two novels coming up. All the delight of making dear friends feel at home for a few hours with promises of another time soon.

In his book, *The Gypsies*, Jan Yoors talks about how a gathering of friends—a half dozen or more gypsy wagons that happened onto a field together—was a time of great celebration, for who knew when such a luxury would come again.

This brings me to wonder if there is anything more wonderful than that peaceful loving time of sharing good food amidst the stories of friends catching up with one another. Maybe it is the simplest of treasures, but treasure it surely is.

Tonight, the dishwasher is chugging, and the woodstove is banked for the night, and sleet and snow continue to fall as Marshall sleeps the sleep of the happy. I have a quiet moment to

Home Life

wonder before slipping in beside him. I think of my dear ones far off in other places and hope they are well. Hope they too have this luxury with dear ones at home.

# First Fire

This morning I built the first fire of this autumn in the woodstove. Now, as I sit trying to clear the email inbox of 1,056 messages, I look out and realize that the large maple that shadows two acres of field is turning more gold each day. I hear the log splitter at the farm churning its force to split several cords of wood. I imagine the basil in our garden wondering when I'm going to get in that pesto mood. The blueberry patch down at the far end of the slope is turning a bright red. Marmalade, Hattie's big gold cat, just took a seat on a lawn chair to watch for field mice. The late flowers enjoy the cool air and know they will soon bow their heads for the last time.

There is a rhythm to this little house in winter. Each morning the window quilts go up to reveal the day, the fire is stoked in the woodstove, and the greenhouse door is opened to heat the house and allow Marshall's camellias some temperate temperatures. The sun is full on the house by 10:30 a.m. and begins to leave the house by 2:30 p.m. in the dead of winter. Oddly, though the hours are short, the angle of the sun—lower in the sky—reaches into our passive solar home twenty-five feet back to the rear wall, heating and fading everything in its path. November and December are the dark months, with an average of ten days of sunlight. In January this changes to bright light for many days and stays that way for the rest of winter.

Today I can feel some of the closing in of summer gone and winter sneaking up, prepared to be so fierce for so long. While the beauty of fall is so striking and wonderful, I always find myself resentful of summer's leaving and almost fearful of the long, dark winter months. I've lived most of my life in New England, and I'm still making peace with winter. How silly.

I wonder about the seasonal changes of spiritual life and nesting: the movement of light as the sun lowers in the sky and reaches farther into the house; the gathering of wood for the deep cold; the filling of the pantry for the winter storm that keeps everyone home; the calls from those in trouble because they have no cozy safe place. These two ideas lie right beside each other: no matter the storm, spring comes again; no matter the trouble, peace comes again.

Home Life

# My Life As a
# Short, Fat, Gay, Italian, Quaker,
# Who Can Yodel

*2011*

Somehow I seem to suddenly have a clearer vision of how I look in the world. Most of my life I have had no idea what I looked like and was too busy with other things to care much. But now I see who I am in the reflections of mirrors, windows, people's eyes with some kind of increased focus. I don't know why I'm noticing it more. It's like seeing myself on YouTube when I'm searching for a video of Pete Seeger. It's an awareness, a self-consciousness that's new to me.

I see myself in a mirror now, and I see the cartoon drawing of an angry old owl—a kind of scowl and furrowed brow and certainly no one I'd want to have lunch with. So I smile at the mirror and try to make improvements. It doesn't seem to change much. Now I'm an angry old owl that is smiling, and even I don't trust it.

It seems part of this change is getting used to being old, or at least older. I'm fifty-nine year and a month old now. I suspect sixty is really going to feel like a cliff edge, and I'll have to take to my bed to let the feelings pass. Later when I notice I haven't died, I'll take a new perspective. Just now and for this next year, I am feeling the gravity around me pulling me in and down, and I'm not that glad about it.

I remember about fifteen or twenty years ago noticing that the path of my life was mostly set. There might be some new adventures and twists and turns, but mainly I was who I was and was, doing what I do and that was that. Most of the story had been written.

There was some relief and some disappointment in noticing this. Relief because I like the life I have and feel like I've chosen well, mostly. I had some disappointment because I didn't want the thrill of new life and adventures to be only for a younger self. I still wanted to travel new ground. There will be some, I hope.

These days new ground makes me feel like I'm huffing and puffing, and I've too little time for new roads and not enough energy for steep climbs. There is already too much to do. Fortunately, it's mostly what I've chosen and what I want, but it is still a bit too much at times.

I like that some parts of my life are spontaneous and in that way I have some luxuries. The phone rings and there's an invitation to teach somewhere out in the world. It goes on the calendar with other invitations, and soon the next year is a web of travel where I'll teach and get my hands on people. It's wonderful.

I also like that I have a small, dull routine when I'm at home that keeps me in low gear, and always preparing for the time when high gear is needed. I get out of bed eventually. I check email, look for the list of things I thought I should get done, maybe do some of them, and check the calendar to see if I am supposed to be anywhere, and often I am working my way through tons of paper on my desk and slowly getting down to the beautiful teak wood surface. Some time in the afternoon I go into town—actually, two towns away—to run errands.

~

I will get the mail at the little Putney Post Office. The staff there is good and friendly. Overheard one day . . .

First lady:  What did the doctor say?

Second lady:  He said not to lift anything heavy.

First lady:  So you're going to stay in bed?

In town I might make copies of handouts for teaching, buy peat moss for the outhouse, shop for groceries finding just the right ingredients for that special something my fine cook husband requests: hot or sweet paprika from Hungary or vanilla beans from Madagascar.

All this is really just an excuse to be in the neighborhood of a thrift store. Why am I mad for second-hand shops? No clue really. I have a few theories: low income for most of my life; I like to find that wonderful something at the very lowest price and take great delight in this. Another idea: to me fine old things are really of another world as a child of the 1950's working-class, first-generation Italian immigrants. A final idea: scanning the shelves of a used goods store is a completely different and relaxing use of the mind after working on the problems of trauma and torture with numerous people. It's as though I take the same mind and not only take it out of gear but put it in another. It becomes a rest in this way. And, there's always the delight of the hunt—can I find the one treasure that is tucked away here?

Home Life

Later on, there's supper with Marshall. If we're lucky he cooks, which is always delicious. Otherwise, I cook, choosing from a small repertoire that tends to avoid lightness. "What do you mean mac-and-cheese with toast and mashed potatoes is heavy? Have some more gravy."

Often in the evening, if we've done the work of checking calendars to see who is leaving on a work trip next, we watch a movie. We don't have TV reception and mainly that's because we find TV boring and dumb. We feel better off without it. But we'll watch a DVD movie. It's not always easy to find good ones.

Then it's 9 or 10 p.m., we go to bed, and I read Marshall to sleep. This takes moments, maybe half a paragraph of a restaurant review and, boom, he's out. Then I put on my bathrobe and sit at my computer ten steps from the bedroom and begin my night's work.

Most nights I do a little email and then go to my list of news websites. I have about twenty-five or thirty now. I usually read eight or ten of them, looking for news about torture. This takes a couple of hours. If I find something that furthers understanding about American torture, I'll share it with the listserve of The Quaker Initiative to End Torture (QUIT). I then print a handout of it for teaching later on. This helps me to know the various parts of torture and know how parts of stories fit together, something quite missing in mainstream media here in the US.

Then to take a break before sleep, I go to the Internet thrift store of my dreams—eBay. Flights of imagination begin by checking out Airstream motorhomes and imagining traveling out of Vermont winter and into a warm desert in the shiny tube home. Then maybe I'll look at Rolls Royces and Bentleys from the 1950's or Citroens from the 1960's, or maybe sailboats. Or maybe I'll look at beach houses for sale. So my mind has moved from torture to imagining delightful things that are fun to see in my mind's eye.

Soon to bed—usually after midnight. I find the *New Yorker* article I've been trying to read and get maybe a page read before I switch off the light and fall asleep. I've a collection of books I try to get through. But reading a whole book is difficult for me. My reading, writing, and learning disabilities are large. Still there are some I work to get through. Lately there's a Pete Seeger biography that is heavy lifting for me.

Several trips around the country each year for the last several decades means I'm often not at home. Still I'm happy for how it's all unfolded, a good life, a bit over full, but with many good choices.

Looking this over, it seems a fairly small and tidy life. Not really very extreme, not until you read some fine print. Like I'm usually helping a dozen people to die in some way or other. My teaching/touching time can be intense. I'm not a primary caregiver, just the one called when there's a sudden burst of fear or pain. All of this has unfolded over time. Some work I wanted to do became a pattern of work over time. The way I've wanted to live in the woods in a small town has become supportive of my work and my comfort when not working. I feel immense gratitude that way has opened for my life to be this way. It's no easy chair, but it fits me well. I'm enjoying the ride and maybe I've saved a few lives—this feels good and important to me.

# Safe Harbor

It is an hour after sunset. Walking up the road, Marshall and I return from supper at the neighbors' farm next door. We are talking about what we might do on vacation at home in two weeks. Then we see her. Slowly grazing her way across the field down by the blueberries, a young doe munches here and there. Her white tail flicking; she is so thin and fragile, so graceful and small, so beautiful in each movement. Slowly looking this way and that, until she comes to the bottom of the slope, far from the house, in the highest grass, near the woods, and lies down. Her head up, slowly watching, and watching. Is this a safe place?

Marshall and I grab the camera and binoculars and head for the big window upstairs. Quietly, quietly, she can hear anything, and we mustn't disturb her. For the longest time, as the light fades, she sits barely visible, surrounded by ferns, slowly turning her head, slowly watching and listening. Is this a safe place? And as dark falls, she lowers her head to sleep.

One of our clearest gay Quakers who died with AIDS, Keith Gann, took the center chair in a grieving circle one year at a Friends General Conference summer gathering. He said that the saddest thing was not the dying—since we'll all do that—but that some of us leave because it's just too hard to stay—the loneliness and inhospitality of the world separate people from us each day, and to leave feeling alone is so sad.

I think of Joe in Los Angeles tonight, and his friend who overdosed. I think of all who seek a safe place to rest from the noise of the world, from the ugliness and lack of reverence, from all of the too-much.

Dear Great and Holy Spirit grant us the safe harbor we need and that we may be that harbor for others each day for all our lives.

# Slightly Murderous

*September 2010*

"Well," says the neighbor to me on a day that's leaving summer and heading toward fall, "you've written another page on your anniversary about your wedding and marriage. Do you realize you've done this every year since God was a child? It's gotten quite boring! We met on the last warm day of summer. *Blah, blah, blah.* Decided to spend the rest of our lives together. *Bore, bore, bore.* Very loving and secure. *Yawn, yawn, yawn.* Fifteen years, eighteen, twenty. Someone make him stop!

"If you really want to write something important, tell us about the hard parts, when all hell breaks loose, when you are not loving and are feeling murderous. That's the important part. That, and how you survive it. How do you bring yourself and each other back from anger and irrational distrust and into harmony? That's worth writing about. All this other schlock is just repeats."

"Well," thinks I, "New Englanders certainly are straightforward, and the task for me here is not to defend but see what parts might be true and go from there. He's right—I've gone on and on each August about true love like some drunk singing in a bar. Can I write what he suggests? Can I write the underbelly of true love and honestly describe the process of learning how to move from murderous to understanding and trusting again? Hmm . . . take a deep breath."

~

The first time I wanted to strangle Marshall was simply a difference in styles. We are frightfully different and alike in so very few ways. As has been my tradition since beginning my traveling work, I clean the house, put everything in order—laundry done and put away, beds made, floors and kitchen and bathroom and desk are clean. Everything is put away in its place and everything does have exactly one place. That's my style, my need, and my way of doing things, living on my own since leaving home at eighteen. This way when I come back home from teaching in some difficult place—a prison, a refugee center, a religious community at odds with itself—I can return to order and beauty and take my rest. But I had neglected to explain this to Marshall and my need to have things tidy upon my return or at least picking up his messes before I returned. So I came home weary and in need of deep rest and walked into the hurricane remains of Marshall leaving everything he touched laying around wherever for the three days of my absence.

Immediately we come to another difference. How does one do anger? I am Italian. My first thought is "Where is my knife?" I begin screaming insults about similarities to certain farm animals. This is normal, John normal. Marshall is WASP Methodist. His first response to his own anger is to deny it and lower his voice. This is Marshall normal. He is educated and ordered in his mind: two masters degrees, a good student, and there is no chaos in his mind. My mind is a cross between a roller coaster and a tornado— external order is necessary because there is none to be had on the inside. I can do more and larger emotions just in the morning than he does in two days. Seems I don't have any small emotions, just big ones, and none of them quiet, none. This is useful when, in your mid-thirties, you're teaching a dozen murdering rapists in prison for life at the same time you're working on healing from incest rape as a young child. Tra-la.

There is also a difference in suspicion and response to pretense. Marshall is truly a nice person. I don't have that problem. I can be nice for brief periods, if it's absolutely necessary; if, say, a prison warden needs reassurance. Marshall tends not to suspect people of anything, no ulterior motives. He makes friends easily. Years ago, this might have meant he'd befriend some sad sack who might try and drain him of all charitable kindness with no resolution in problems ever. He's kind that way. I can help someone, but I am frighteningly honest about *whose trouble is this and who is doing the work on it?—is that clear? This is yours, what are you doing about it? Here's what little I know that might help. Now go home and get to work.* At least this is how I think I see Marshall and me. People come to false fronts, facades, and pretenses quite honestly. Life is hard and everyone needs strategies to get through. One could be patient with these, forgiving and compassionate.

Such things don't bother Marshall who has more social grace and diplomacy than any ten people. False fronts make me nuts, no doubt revealing a lack of mercy with myself for my own pretenses. I have too little grip on reality to hang out with anyone else's nonsense. So I tend to ungraciously call them on it or get rid of them. I mean, invite them out of my life, out of my house, out of all guest lists—a snob in the form of an authenticity nut. There are social functions where Marshall's response is a better choice. Smile, nod, and don't say a thing. Some do this so well. Such exercise just makes me imagine going out and killing small animals.

So what do we do with these differences? It seems the first thing we do, when we discover a new gulf in style, actions or beliefs, is to let the other one know something is not right. Marshall will lower his voice to emphasize its importance. I, on the other hand, will yell and scream, a matter of sincerity in my tribal communications. After this first failure of communication and understanding, we can proceed to seeing how each holds his perspective, the how and why of the pieces in our contrasting lives and patterns. We learned to lay these out like unfolding a road map, seeing he thought we were over here and me thinking we were certainly over there, and lo, both have some truth and both perspectives need the other to be complete. I hate not being right. Being humble when I make mistakes seems to cause pain. But slowly I learned that I can be wrong and the world can go on without anyone's life being threatened—a reality I grew up with that dissipates too slowly. Marshall's gift for being nice becomes invaluable at these times. He can soothe me in ways I never knew before. It is the best loving of all.

Marshall is particularly good at gracious living. He's an excellent cook and has great taste in color, design, and style. He is also very widely educated in the liberal arts. He knows how religion, art, and food are expressed differently by various peoples throughout history. He has great overview and particulars in many aspects of human history and reads voraciously. I don't. But I can tell you why someone has a certain posture as they schlep through the airport or why that certain personality we met last night in the form of a college administrator has a blind spot that spoils all good work. This makes us useful, one at a time in various settings.

When there is an emergency and everyone else is in shock and motionless, I already have a plan of action and am directing necessary steps. Whether this is a natural disaster or a death in the family, I'm ready with an overview, perceiving individual needs, and whether professionals are needed before others have caught a second breath. The absence of emergency situations used to get a little boring for me. When there were no edges in a group of people, it felt somehow lacking. But I can pretend such things are normal and stop tapping my foot waiting for the crisis that doesn't come. In this way we are actually a good pair. If there's harmony, we can take Marshall's style and live the good life. If all hell breaks loose, I'm the best dinner guest since Marcus Welby. We each understand these stances as ministry in our own lives.

Marshall has been shy to learn about power. I did my graduate work in power at age seven. I've had occasion to offer Marshall opportunity to step out into his power and observe imbalances of power in certain systems and how that might be worked with. I have been slow to trust and be tender in this marriage. I needed some years and a certain setting before I really and truly unpacked and live with this other person. I wanted someone who could protect me. Actually, Marshall can't do that. He can't become someone else, butch up, and tell someone off or stop insult, assault, or deceit. But he can love me beyond what I ever knew to be possible. This creates a new reality wherein I don't need to be as protected as I had thought. I can now also surrender to tenderness and allow myself to be taken care of like that unicorn under the tree, no longer skittish and squirrely. So, what seem to be aggravating opposites are actually balancing acts that need to be joined, occasions for learning and unfolding.

In the years before so much of this was understood, it seemed impossibly difficult for me to bear any pain that might come from the one I know loves me most in the world. How could this be? How come I still get hurt? Didn't I surrender to love enough? Didn't we promise to take of care one another?

I can't bear pain from something he's done. But a few breaths later and it's clear that yes, indeed, I do hurt and it's logical that I'm having this response to something that he's done. Lo, there was nothing intentional about the hurt. Is it any help to know this?

Well, frankly, not at first. So, I take a few breaths, stop looking for my knife, and wonder about these parts from his perspective. This is easier to do when I am rested and have no backlog of grief or anger that are in process. After all, what is life but a series of deep emotions, tearing through, and mostly understood later?

All this knowing has taken years and decades to smooth out. Our annoyances now tend to be the smaller known variety, to which my first thought is, "May all our troubles be this size!" The task all along seems to be unfolding toward our best selves, becoming more of who we are—that bright shining essence that first drew us toward one another.

And, of course, there are still the parts that don't fit easily. Marshall would rather forego a meal than eat poorly and go without rather than buy inferior things. I do not forego meals; fast food is not really food, but at least I stop being hungry. And making do with used rather than new is nearly religion in my thrift store karma experience. When I found him a $100 Nambe dish for 25 cents in the pie tin stack, there was a growing appreciation for what might be possible.

The one I love most can be the channel for the most learning, because it's here that I'm most engaged, and most trusting, and most watchful. It's here that conflict can hurt the most. I don't mean intended hurt—which only happens in an on-going way as pathology—but rather misunderstanding or not quite enough care or simply not knowing enough or not having shared enough. Feeling slightly murderous, even for a short time, can mean that the connections are deep and important.

After all, love should be a little scary. It's not like it's lying all around free for the taking and easy to do. It's important enough to have some reverence for, but also powerful enough that it needs the respect one has for barbed wire as fencing. We go carefully, because we are each fragile beings handling powerful things.

Now have I painted a picture of us that is extreme and unbelievable? Is Marshall a cultured pushover and I an emotional schitzo not allowed near sharp things? Does this give some balance in the accounting of who we are? Aren't we all really too much to try and show on a page? Did I tell you that while Marshall usually has one appointment to create a wedding cake on his calendar, I am usually helping several people to die? See? It's just more so at every layer.

# The Turkey & the Saw

*January 25, 2007*

*Well . . . I just want to say that if by chance*

你 just happened to pull an old circular saw out of the
rubbish that your departing landlord had discarded when he
sold you the house,

and you found this saw to be only a little dangerous because of
this-and-that wear and tear

and 17 years later the prep school on the hill,
where your friend and neighbor was raising turkeys,
but had forgotten to book the butcher in advance and several of
these turkeys became quite large before their day of reckoning,

and he asked you to buy one as a favor before they outgrew
the cow barn,

*and that turkey was larger than any pan you owned*

and borrowing the neighbor's pan where twelve-for-dinner
means most of the family is out,
and, lo, that pan did not fit into your oven,

*Well . . . it just might be*

that you could take that 40-pound turkey

and wedge it into the kitchen sink . . .

and then use the circular saw to cut that sucker in half,

much to the disgust of your husband . . .

*who really did grow up in a much more proper family than yours*

where they never had the occasion for flying turkey meat

to be landing on the ceiling like sawdust,

but more sticky.

# Thanksgiving 2001

Late night, Thanksgiving eve. The frosty air is chilling the moonlit night. Marshall and John Meyer are hard at work in the kitchen making pumpkin and apple pies for tomorrow, having already creamed the onions, braised the cabbage, sauced the cranberries, and butterflied and brined the huge turkey. I've set a table for six over a huge plywood board covered by a freshly ironed linen tablecloth. Surmounting this, a maze of cobalt Fiesta ware from years of thrift store collecting, crystal from Marshall's Aunt Ramona, and silver from his Grandma Ruth. Tomorrow Chuck, Kenneth, and David will arrive to make a full compliment of every manner of gay Quaker man.

I notice two things as I find just the right platter for white meat and another for dark meat. I wonder when my priorities moved from having a VW bus and a Martin guitar to having enough linen napkins for everyone? How happy I am to be making the house beautiful and having Marshall in the kitchen dreaming up a new way to make gravy. One year it was champagne, cream, and fresh jalapeno!

Going out for a moment into the cold night, I say a prayer for all those who don't have joy and safety. I say a prayer for everyone who can't get home, for all who are sick, imprisoned, alone, being hurt, afraid, and without hope for tomorrow. I send this out into the night, so glad to be home.

Home Life

*Menu ~ Thanksgiving November 22, 2001*

*John & Marshall, Chuck, David, Kenneth, John*
~~~~~~~~~~~~~~~~~~~~~~~~~~
*International Cheese Fantasia*
*Oak Smoked Cheddar*
*Leroule with Garlic & Herbs*
*Shropshire Bleu Cropwell Bishop*
*Bucheron*
*Olives Provencal*
*Coppola Carbernet Sauvignon 1999*

~

*Butterflied Roast Turkey*
*Buttermilk Garlic Riced Potatoes*
*Traditional Bread Stuffing*
*Braised Red Cabbage*
*Pickled Onions*
*Steamed Broccoli*
*Spinach Salad with Clementine Dressing*
*Pear Gingered Cranberry Sauce*

~

*Spiced Pumpkin Pie*
*Cortland-MacIntosh Pie crème Courvoisier*

~

*Prosecco Di Conegliano Carpene Malvolti*
*Chandone Brut Classic Champagne*
*Pinot Blanc Trimbach*
*Chardonnay Steele Cuvee 1999*

# Hospitality and Healing

One of the great things about healing is providing hospitality. Healing relies on some worthy person to offer a trusting relationship to the wounded. Hospitality can be shown in any number of ways. It might be someone who listens well and is not afraid to hear your story. Or it might be someone who is simply glad to see you. And perhaps most universally, it is the making of good food and a warm welcome to the table.

Compassionate work is largely a work of hospitality. Making someone welcome at a critical time may be an important comfort and a relief. It can be the beginning of a deeper trust leading to the deeper work of healing. We are being hospitable when we offer travelers something they need. Every wounded person is traveling a path where much is needed. Who makes welcome in our lives? Who feels the generosity of spirit and well-being enough to share that feeling with others as a cloak to share, as dry ground to stand on after some horrible event has come? This is beyond optimism and toward a love of life and a belief that things can be made better, pain and confusion made less.

My grandmother had a large family and was very welcoming to anyone who came to the farm. I never saw anyone turned away from the table or from needing a place to sleep. That's the kind of welcome I was surrounded with and it was lifesaving. It's also a standard I try to keep in my own ways.

I remember that table being full of wonderful things made on the farm. I grew up on homemade bread, butter, and jams. We had our own eggs, milk, cheese, and meats. Sunday dinners, when many of grandmother's children returned to the farm bringing their children, were crowded and fun. And the food was always good and plentiful. There were seasonal favorites, many stories told, and always plenty.

I've included some favorite recipes here as a way of sharing hospitality and connecting it with healing. Being welcomed, having a place, knowing there is plenty of what is needed—all are vital to healing from trauma and to good village life in general.

When one of my beloveds is hurting, I not only want to touch to heal, I also want to offer rest, comfort, and good food. And when there is no crisis, welcome and plenty are good ways to live, to view life, and to know life's beauty even amidst hardship.

Here are three recipes that are old favorites from home. I hope you will find them useful in making welcome wherever you are.

Home Life

# Sauce and Meatballs

My mother, Carmela Martha Naples Calvi, had short-term memory loss in her later years. We couldn't talk about yesterday or last year. So we talked about her father buying the farm in Durham, Connecticut, in 1925. They came with horse and wagon and gas engine vehicles. She talked about building her house in the 1940's on the north border of the family farm where her father had raised pigs. Mostly, we talked about food and I wrote down some recipes.

At her funeral, one of my cousins said, "She made the best spaghetti sauce in the world. . . . You did get that recipe, didn't you?"

Here's the way she taught me to make spaghetti sauce and meatballs. This recipe yields eight servings. Make sure you have everything on hand before you start; prepare the sauce first.

Measurements are personal things, and handfuls or sprinkles depend on taste.

# Carmela's Spaghetti Sauce

## Utensils

Large stockpot with lid

A boning knife for peeling tomatoes and a paring knife for slicing garlic

## Ingredients

10 large beefy tomatoes

Olive oil, enough to generously cover bottom of stockpot

5 large garlic cloves

Small handful of raisins

Large handful of chopped fresh basil

Large sprinkle of dried oregano

Salt and pepper

Optional: a splash of red wine or dry Vermouth, orange peel, cloves, sautéed onion, fresh chopped parsley

## Preparation

1. Peel, seed, and chop 10 large tomatoes. To peel, dunk in boiling water for 10 seconds, then peel, seed, and chop. (Or cheat with canned tomatoes.)

2. Cover the bottom of a stockpot with olive oil and bring to a simmer. The oil should shimmer and look slightly wavy.

3. Peel and finely slice 5 large garlic cloves, add to simmering oil.

4. Add a small handful of raisins.

5. Add tomatoes to stockpot.

6. Add a large handful of fresh basil chopped; leaves not stems.

7. Add a large sprinkle of oregano and simmer 2 to 4 hours, stirring often and gently.

8. Salt and pepper to taste.

9. Add optional ingredients to taste.

# Carmela's Meatballs

## Utensils

Large bowl for preparing meatballs

Large heavy skillet

## Ingredients

1 pound each ground beef, ground pork, ground veal

4 to 5 slices homemade bread, chopped, soaked in water or milk—or use dry bread crumbs generously

Handful of chopped fresh basil

Large sprinkle of dried oregano

Handful of raisins

Handful of chopped fresh parsley

1 cup Parmesan cheese

½ cup roasted, coarsely-ground pine nuts

Salt and pepper to taste

Half-cup of olive oil or enough to coat the pan

Makes 18 to 20 two-inch meatballs

Preparation

1. Mix all ingredients in large mixing bowl with your hands and shape mixture into 2-inch balls.

2. Brown the meat balls in a skillet turning enough so all sides brown and the insides are cooked; best way to know is by sampling.

3. Slip meatballs carefully into stockpot of simmering tomato sauce.

4. Simmer a while, taste test, and eat as soon as the pasta is ready.

# Making Bread

My uncle, John Naples, for whom I'm named, taught his nieces and nephews how to make bread. This could only happen at night, as he was busy with the farm all day. His gift for eccentricity grew in his old age and intrigued us young children. He would dress up in a completely white outfit of sweat pants, sweat shirt, socks, sneakers and chef hat. No one else in the family had ever heard of bread-making outfits. His love of language meant using more large words than necessary and enjoying it. Where anyone else would say, "Where's the butter?" Uncle John would say, "Can someone please enlighten me as to the whereabouts of the butter?"

There was serious hand washing and merciless scrubbing of all surfaces and tools. As the family was large, bread was mixed in a large wide metal basin that held dough for 10 loaves. This bread pan was used for nothing else and had a place of honor and reverence in the kitchen. After all was mixed, kneaded, and set to rise, he taught us to pray over the bread, prayers of thanksgiving and for those without bread. It was a class in ethics, reverence, and aesthetics along with cooking. I follow all these rules decades later, enjoying the feel of dough almost as much as the taste of good homemade bread.

My dear friend and co-conspirator, Bill Kreidler, and I both taught young children in classrooms for many years. This is a recipe Bill used in his classroom for kids to make their own bread. It's simple, quick, and delicious.

Home Life

# Bill's French Bread

Makes 2 small loaves

| Utensils | Ingredients |
|---|---|
| Measuring cup | 1-1/2 cups warm water |
| Measuring spoons | 1 tablespoon honey, warmed |
| Large mixing bowl | 1/2 tablespoon salt |
| Sharp knife | 1 packet dried yeast |
| Small bread pans or a cookie sheet | 4 cups flour |

Preparation

1. Combine very warm water—110-115° F, salt, honey, and yeast in a large bowl.

2. Let mixture rest, uncovered, for about 10 minutes while the yeast activates.

3. Add all of the flour slowly to the mixture, working it in until there are no dry or wet parts but equally moist.

4. Shape loaves and let rise for 20 minutes covered on a board.

5. Heat oven to 450° F.

6. Using a sharp knife, make a slash in the top of the loaf...or carve your initials.

7. Bake 20 minutes.

8. Let cool or cool off until just warm and enjoy with butter melting under strawberry or elderberry jam.

Home Life

# Section 8

# Healing America, Ending Torture

FRIENDS GENERAL CONFERENCE

Grinnell College, Grinnell, Iowa

2011

| | |
|---|---|
| Introduction to Plenary | 201 |
| To Go Where There is No Light | 203 |
| End Notes to Section 8 | 215 |

# Introduction to Plenary

My name is Callie Marsh, from the West Branch Friends Meeting of Iowa Yearly Meeting, Conservative.

It's my great pleasure this evening to introduce to you John Calvi. There are many stories about John. About his teaching massage in prisons, stories about healing touch with refugees, stories about his wedding to Marshall Brewer under the care of the Putney Friends Meeting in Vermont in August of 1989. John has asked me to share a few of those stories with you.

*From a Friend in Philadelphia.* "My friend, Susan, was dying and several of us gathered in her downstairs living room in silent worship. Upstairs her partner, Karen, and Susan's mother attended her. Susan was not really conscious and was struggling in the last hours. Karen called John Calvi and held the phone to Susan's ear. I don't know what he told her, but she calmed down and had a peaceful death later that day. Everyone downstairs could feel that shift from struggle to peace. It was clearly a gift of the Spirit."

*Another story, from one of John's cousins.* "One summer's day as we were playing on grandmother's farm, a few of us young cousins fell into a patch of nettles. And it was stinging our hands. John took us down to the brook and covered our hands in mud to cool them. And after washing in the cold water, he put on the clear salve of the Jewelweed. The pain stopped right then. How could he know such a thing at five years old?"

John has had a life's work as a Quaker healer. His traveling ministry began with a survivor of torture in 1982. He is well known among Friends General Conference with his workshops since 1987. Raise your hand if you've been in his workshop.

[Callie aside to John: I hardly feel a *need* to introduce you.]

It's often, and you know this, the largest workshop and the one to fill up first. In 2005 John asked a small group of Friends to help him bring Friends together for a conference on torture. John became the founding convener of the Quaker Initiative to End Torture. QUIT. The Light that John has been given has been well used as a comfort to many, and he has been faithful to his gift.

John will speak out of the silence on the healing of America by ending torture.

# To Go Where There is No Light

*John speaks out of the silence.*

*Dear Great and Holy Spirit, be with me now as I do this work that there may be comfort and healing and protection.*

Friends, I am so honored to be invited to speak with you this evening. I am grateful for all the good work that goes into every Gathering to bring us here all together in this nomadic community of Friends. And I am grateful that on stage with me tonight is most of the original group that formed the Quaker Initiative to End Torture, both the steering committee and elders who held us in prayer. Most are here with us tonight.

Friends have a wonderful history of doing work in the world which is nearly impossible. It's one of the things we love about our history. We love that Margaret Fell said, "We're going to go into that prison and shine God's love upon them." We love that we were part of the Underground Railroad. We love that John Woolman would excuse himself from the grand parlors of talking with the owners and go and eat with the servants. This wonderful history of people taking on large work, which at the beginning seemed impossible, completely impossible! Too large to do! We love that there is contemporary history and stories of people doing good works. Of Jim Corbett with the Sanctuary Movement. Of Lawrence Aspey and Stephen Angell with the Alternatives to Violence Project. Beautiful work. Bayard Rustin with the March on Washington.

In Newark, New Jersey, Bonnie Kerness, doing prison work with AFSC, who came out with a book in the last year that she helped to edit to teach people in prison how to survive solitary confinement. A nearly impossible work.

Now, of course, at the beginning of each one of these works, it was not a popular idea. When Margaret Fell said, "We have to go into that prison" not everyone said, "Okay, Meg, I'll get the picnic basket." No. It was just a few unreasonable people of great faith. The Light was so bright they couldn't not go.

Then what happens is the Light starts to get brighter, and more people start to see it. More people cannot resist that bright Light and the work grows larger and more people come to the work. Eventually, eventually, we say, "We were all there!"

It's sort of the Woodstock syndrome. You know, only about 300,000 folks were, and now 3 million people are sure they were there.

Tonight I want to talk about an impossible work, an impossible work.

This time we can be at the beginning of it, together. A lot of us.

One of the things that makes a perfect spiritual work is that it stretches you. It brings you some new life-giving energy, because you are experiencing a connection with the Divine and an experience of living hope. You use all of your talents. You use all of your skills and learn some new ones. You find out there are some things you can do that you had no idea, no idea, that you were going to do.

New work should stretch but not break a person. We don't want there to be any more injury or any more overload. We don't want one more Quaker doing too much. We want to learn surrender and humility. We want to understand that as we go to do good works in the world, maybe the first job is not to change the world. Maybe the first work is to come closer to the Divine. Maybe that is the reason to choose a large spiritual work—to be at one with our words; to be at one with belief. We come to this new place of understanding as to what is truly important.

Of course, large spiritual work will break your heart—you will witness things that you can't change, you can't fix. This breaking of the heart is a vital part of large spiritual work because it is the last boundary of understanding our common humanity. When we weep, we weep not only for our own sadness, we join in the grief of the world that anyone is treated so horribly. We grieve that there can be so much loss of dignity and humanity for anyone.

Let's consider American torture. I'm not going to tell you the worst stories. There are lots of them. I'm just going to give you a quick outline of some of what used to be and some of what is.

Now, of course, in the United States torture has *always* been against the law. Remember the phrase "cruel and unusual punishment?" The idea that some punishment could be too much was being debated in Europe when our founding fathers were considering what rights were necessary. They said, "Sounds like a good idea. Maybe we don't have to cut people in half in the town square to get them to obey the laws. Maybe we could just put them in jail. We don't have to be mean and stupid; we can just be hard on them."

And so this became part of the Bill of Rights, which became the first group of amendments to the United States Constitution.

Conversely, of course, America has always used torture. In every one of its wars and to maintain slavery, for instance. And so we have lived all of our life as a nation with this dichotomy. It's wrong and against the law, and we have used it. We have used it, trying to use it without talking about it.

When the OSS was changing into the CIA after World War II, there was a decision to study mind control, and, later on, to study torture. Information was purchased from people who had carried out torture experiments. Information was purchased from Russian doctors who were doing torture experiments in World War II, and from Nazi doctors, and later on from the Israeli Mossad. All of this information was brought together, and then further experiments were done. Many different kinds of experiments were done. Eventually they perfected torture. The perfection of torture has been an American creation.

Here's the main thing that was discovered. It is not physical pain which is the greatest torture. That will not gain you control of everyone. The most effective torture is to orchestrate a very delicate ballet between overwhelming senses and underwhelming the senses.

The play between light and dark. The play between being too hot and too cold. The play between feeling safe and not feeling safe. Being allowed to sleep and not being allowed to sleep. Being allowed to eat and not being allowed to eat. Being allowed to be clothed and not being allowed to be clothed.

When these techniques are combined and used together, you can gain control of someone fairly quickly. What it accomplishes is the deconstruction of the human personality, so that a person no longer trusts his or her own senses.

The Quaker Initiative to End Torture (QUIT) exhibit table has all of the stories I'm going to tell tonight; we have written documentation of all of the stories. We also have a brief but incisive history of torture written by Alfred McCoy, J. R. W. Smail Professor of History at the University of Wisconsin, Madison. I've made copies of that for you all to take home to your Meetings.

Now within all of this, there are jokes about torture. But none are funny, because what they do is to prove the meanness and the stupidity of torture. Here's a torture joke from World War II.

Joseph Stalin complained to his secretary at breakfast that his silver-handled comb had been stolen from his bedroom, and that the thief had to be found. When he came back at lunch, he said to his secretary that the comb had only fallen behind his bureau and so the search could be called off. And the secretary said, "But sir, twelve people have already confessed."

Jokes about torture, like jokes about rape, are simply not funny. Rape, of course, is the oldest torture. It is the most common torture.

Let me talk about our current situation with torture.

We have in our midst several different economies engaged in the business of America being at war. One of those economies is torture. It takes a great deal of money to torture people, because if you want to torture someone, you have to kidnap them. You know, that's called "extraordinary rendition." But you have to kidnap someone. If you want to kidnap someone, you have to grab them secretly and you have to fly them away secretly. So you need a private jet and you need a private pilot and a private landing strip. And you need a private prison. All of this costs a great deal of money. And because it's secret, a great deal more is charged.

One aspect of ending American torture would be to end this clandestine economy.

Here's another fact about current American torture. Remember the picture from Abu Ghraib of the fellow with the hood in a poncho standing on a box? He has wires dangling from his fingers. It was one of the first pictures out of Abu Ghraib. And we were told that there were a few bad apples in the prison who had done this. We were assured America was not engaged in something like this. Well, in torture circles, do you know what that position is called? It's called the Viet Nam position, because it was invented by the Phoenix Program of the CIA during the American war in Viet Nam.

Another piece of the torture picture is the torture of children. I have to confess to you that this is work I never wanted to do. I tried real hard to get out of it. I had been working with tortured refugees for about 20 years when the pictures from Abu Ghraib came out, and I knew that Friends had to come together and do some work. And I called all the large Quaker organizations, and they all said, "You're absolutely right. But we have no time or money for such a thing. If you start something, we'll help you." Now I'm already traveling around the country several times a year working by invitation, living mainly on gifts, and I simply didn't have time for a second job. But then I went to a presentation and found out that the youngest prisoner was a seven-year-old girl who had been tortured.

Americans imprisoning children. Americans torturing children. God help us.

The next day I called up five friends and they said, "Yes we'll work with you." So in June of 2005 the Quaker Initiative to End Torture was born.

There are a number of things that don't come through our news media. Very few people know that there were so many children at Guantánamo prison that there had to be a second camp opened up—Camp Iguana. Now why would we snatch a child away from Afghanistan and bring him or her to Guantánamo? Partly because you hold that child up in front of the cell of the father and say, "If you don't tell us everything you know, think about what we're going to do to your child." And then that child is hurt down the hall so the father can hear the screams.

This might be a good time to pause. Take a breath. I apologize. Put your feet flat on the floor. Loosen up your fingers. I know you're all squinched up out there. Me too.

~

We're told that waterboarding is simulated drowning and doesn't really hurt. The fact of the matter is that we have eyewitness accounts of people drowning during waterboarding and doctors resuscitating them. They are then waterboarded again. Can you imagine dying more than once in a day by drowning?

One of the fellows who was in the White House, a legal counsel, wrote the rules for waterboarding, to show that it was a perfectly reasonable thing to do. He was made a federal judge in the southwest United States, a Federal judgeship. Some time later a case came to him when he was on a panel of judges. A young seminary student from California, as part of his service, would go and leave gallon jugs of water in the desert for people who were crossing from Mexico so they wouldn't die from dehydration. The border guards arrested him and put him in jail, but they didn't know what to charge him with, because saving a life is not yet against the law. So they decided they would charge him with littering. Two of the judges on the panel said, "This is nonsense. Throw this case out and shame on you for bringing it." But the third judge, Jay Bybee, who had written the rules on what made waterboarding legal, said, "Oh no, this is absolutely against the law."

This is one of the ironies we run into.

There's another story from Guantánamo. In 2007 a group of lawyers came together, lawyers for the detainees in Guantánamo, and said, "We have all of these people and they're going crazy. They must be going crazy because this is a hopeless situation. They're not being charged. They're not being allowed to see evidence against them. They're not being allowed to contact lawyers or family. And there's no way for them to get out of here. This must be what's driving them crazy."

And then earlier this year we found out what really was making them crazy. Back when the Guantánamo Bay Detention Camp opened in January of 2002, the first 420 detainees were given an antimalarial medicine. They were given the worst anti-malarial medicine, and it is the worst because it causes depression, psychosis, and suicidal thoughts. They were given five times the normal dosage. Then their vital signs were taken for the next year. Every day. This is medical experimentation and is contrary to the principles known as the Nuremberg Code written by Americans at the Nuremberg trials.

There's another story that came out a while ago. You know we were told that the fellows in Guantánamo, almost 800 of them, were the worst of the worst. Then later we found out that they weren't captured on the battlefield trying to kill our brave soldiers, they were turned in for a bounty. Who got turned in for the bounty? Let's say your children were sick and needed medicine in Afghanistan, where the average annual income is $700, and you could get a bounty of $5,000. People turned in their brother-in-law who they didn't like. They turned in the landlord they owed money to. They turned in the fellow down the road because no one cared about him. By and by after a great deal of torture it became clear that these were people who knew nothing. The vast majority of the 800 had no information.

President Bush and Vice-President Cheney sat down in discussion in the White House to decide whether or not the people should be sent back to where they came from. They discussed whether the prisoners should be released. The decision was made that they could not be released because the congress had not yet granted permission for the Iraq war, and they did not want to appear to have made a mistake and thereby slow the movement toward war.

So innocent people were kept for years.

There are more stories, such as those about force-feeding. On the third day of his presidency, President Barack Obama gave an executive order that there was to be no more torture, no more waterboarding. Three months later the new attorney general flew down to Guantánamo to collect the legal files and see what could be done with the fellows who were there. What could possibly be done? The military commission tribunals were clearly illegal, and many were halted. And now they wanted to see if there was some other choice that could be invented.

As the attorney general was there collecting those files, a military lawyer defending a detainee—on her own dime—flew to England to beg the government of the United Kingdom to take back one of the Guantánamo prisoners who held a British passport. She said, "You have to take him back, otherwise with the treatment he is receiving, he will not survive." So clearly we are not adhering to the Geneva Conventions or Red Cross recommendations if people are dying in custody. The prisoner was dying in custody because he was on a hunger strike. Hunger strikers were then force fed, and if they resisted forced feeding, they were beaten. Both beatings and forced feedings are contrary to the intent of the Geneva Conventions.

All of the Bush appointed lawyers in the Justice Department that argued against any possibility of justice for those detainees are still in the Justice Department, still making arguments against any rights for those detainees.

Unfortunately, I must report that with this new presidency almost nothing has changed with regards to American torture. Some things have changed on the outside, but very little on the inside.

There is another concern that may be even more frightening. At a recent anniversary of publication of the Pentagon Papers of 1971, Daniel Ellsberg said that all of the items in the Articles of Impeachment brought forth by the House Judiciary Committee against President Nixon are now legal. All legal.

So in terms of stopping American torture, the first question that comes up is: What parts of the democracy are still working? If we want to stop American torture, what are the venues open to us to make that change?

Last September all of the large anti-torture organizations came together in Washington, D.C.: Amnesty International, the Carter

Center, Human Rights Watch to End Torture, the Quaker Initiative to End Torture, the National Religious Campaign Against Torture. And there was consensus that the White House, the congress, and the courts are all closed. All closed to Americans requesting the end of torture, requesting investigation, requesting prosecutions.

When a country is involved in crimes against humanity, there is an inevitable sequence of events: the crimes take place and then the country works very hard to turn numbness into amnesia. The event or events become a nightmare which passed, and which is no longer discussed. It's no longer part of national conversation. And what QUIT would like to do, and the other organizations are working to do, is to keep the conversation alive.

Very soon after QUIT was organized, we had a web site, we had publications, we had speakers, we had conferences, we had a list-serve—all with the idea of keeping Friends informed about what is happening with regard to American torture. Now it is absolutely vital that we learn and remember the stories, and keep asking the questions . . . because what happens is, if the spiritual community brings an issue to the front, that amnesia wears off. The amnesia wears off and, by and by, questions are asked, and investigations are made. We have seen this in South Africa, in Chile, in Argentina, in El Salvador. We can do that in the United States of America.

And when I say that, I also want to tell you that I think it's going to take at least two generations of Quakers to accomplish. Two generations of Quakers to accomplish. It's no less work than slavery; it's no less work than women's suffrage. I think it's going to take two generations because torture is so interwoven in the structures of government, the business of war. If this happens, it will be the first time in the history of our country that high leadership will be brought to accountability for crimes against humanity. The first time.

Then you know what's logically next? Taking the United States out of the business of war. Of course. We start with torture because torture is the most offensive. It is the most obscene. It is the arena where we find the greatest agreement that this piece of the business of war should not be taking place and that the people who made decisions to engage in torture should be brought to accountability. It's not a matter of mere confessions about what happened in the past; it's still going on. Money is still being made. Fortunes are being made on torture. The School of the Americas, now renamed as the Western Hemisphere Institute for Security Cooperation (WHINSEC), has now trained over 60,000 people in torture.

So in part what I'm asking from you tonight is to take part in the healing of America. Each one of us wants to love our country, dearly, as family, as a very large family, as a collection of ideas and principles that we hold sacred and with great reverence. There needs to be a washing. There needs to be a cleansing. There needs to be great reverence brought to this work.

Now the reason this needs to be a spiritual work is because . . . it's horrible. Kids, it is horrible. It's just horrible.

This work is not for human beings alone. Not for mere human beings. This has got to be done with spiritual disciplines and with great Light, and with an understanding that there is a divine connection asking for this healing to take place. Asking that humanity be washed and carry Light where no light has been for a very long time.

The Quaker Initiative to End Torture asks you to learn these stories, to invite us to speak to your Monthly Meetings, Quarterly Meetings, and Yearly Meetings. We ask you to download information from our website. To join our listserve. To come to our conferences and share this information with people in your Meeting, and share some context with which to understand the stories and to know that there is a way to stop this, that there is a way to end this.

Chuck Fager is part of a group in North Carolina that did some work to see if there was torture in their state. They checked out private landing strips. Someone took down the tail numbers of the planes they saw that matched the tail numbers of planes that had been noted in Europe as being part of the torture taxi network, extraordinary rendition.

Do you have private airstrips in your state?

Do you have prisons in your state?

American torture has migrated into our domestic prisons. The use of stun guns is common. Of increasing concern is the overuse of solitary confinement—one of the fastest ways to make it impossible for someone to be a sociable human being. People are spending very long periods of time in solitary confinement for very small offenses. This is a change in the American prison system, which is truly ruining people's lives so they can never reform, never live independently again. They will become permanent wards of the state, dependents of the state.

Do you have prisons in your area of the country doing this? Do you know the chaplain there? Does your Meeting have a relationship with a local prison?

QUIT is not a regular Quaker organization. We did not come together through a clearness committee; we were not recommended and suggested to go forward by a Yearly Meeting. We were a bunch of unreasonable people who were basically like a bunch of kids saying, "Let's build a tree house!" And we did. Many Meetings have joined us. We have minutes from thirty-three Yearly Meetings, Monthly Meetings, and Quarterly Meetings. They support this work and have joined it. We don't operate as a group of people telling you what to do. We operate as a group of people saying, "Here's a story we know. We would like for you to create a response that will contribute to the flow of energy and Light."

One Quaker Meeting rented a billboard with a quote from Matthew 5:44, "Love your enemies," and a picture of a detainee bound, hooded, and handcuffed. The caption said, "Does this look like love?" It just happened to be on one of the most scenic highways where everyone who wanted to see the beautiful fall colors would be reminded.

What might be possible within your Meeting? Is there someone in your Meeting who could collect stories and have a small billboard posted? Is there a small group that could be had in your Meeting just to share information with other people? The Quaker Initiative to End Torture is also soliciting donations. We need some more people to join us on the steering committee. Currently the steering committee is myself, Chuck Fager, and Scilla Wahrhaftig. And look at Scilla, there she is on the end, coughing. Who's got a jug of water for Scilla? Yes? Look at her. She's almost seventy years old. Chuck, for god's sake is almost seventy years old. They're old! Now me, I'm only tired!

We need some new folks. We need some folks with experience, and we need some young folks. We need people who are also going to join us, who are going to take up the torch, and keep this work going. We have talked to dozens of Monthly Meetings and Yearly Meetings, and we want to do much more. But we need your help.

Friends have always been called to find the worst situation and figure out what is needed there. A good friend of mine who went to do some Quaker work at the end of World War II, and his first job, as a twenty-two year old man, was to go into one of the concentration camps and sort out the living from the dead. It was his first job as a Quaker. And we have this lovely anticipation that each person who comes to Quakerism is going to go on a spiritual adventure. And it's going to be some manner of service that's not only going to teach you things but it's going to change you.

And so I'm asking you tonight to ponder this concern about American torture. Have you something to offer? Have you a gift to bring?

When Margaret Fell went into prison for refusing to take an oath in 1664, she had no concern that she might end up dying in prison. She was listening closely to her Light. She knew she was making the right choices. In my work as a Quaker healer it is common for people's pain to pass through me. One of the first tortured refugees I worked on was a young man from Iran. Ali been tortured for being a Christian and was put in prison. He escaped, jumped on a boat, came to New York, and jumped into the harbor. The United States would not give him sanctuary, and he went to Canada, where he found the home of Nancy Pocock, a great Quaker lady who took in refugees and tried to get them asylum. She said to me, "I want you to work with Ali, who's only eighteen years old. He's been through a great deal. I think we can get him asylum. I had to talk the newspaper into not using his last name because his family is still at home and they could be tortured."

And as Ali lay on the massage table, and my hands grew warm, the pain passed out of him, and through me, and out. He looked up at me with tears in his eyes and said, "This is how my body felt before, before the hurt."

We can all of us, we *can*—all of us, bring America back to that time before the hurt. We can end American torture.

There's going to come a time when if you want to find out about torture you'll have to read about it in a history book. That's going to be a beautiful day. I don't think I'll see it. But I would like to see that work become very large and beautiful.

I'd like to close with a blessing, that there be a blessing on everyone who can't get home tonight, that there be blessings on everyone who's in pain, that there be a blessing on everyone who's in danger, or being hurt, or hurting.

*Dear great Holy Spirit, thank you for this day and for this work. Thank you for these Friends and for these lives. Please wash me and help me to be ready for more.*

# End Notes to Section 8

In this talk about torture and the Quaker Initiative to End Torture, John says: "The Quaker Initiative to End Torture (QUIT) exhibit table has all of the stories I'm going to tell tonight; we have written documentation of all of the stories. We also have a brief but incisive history of torture written by Alfred McCoy, J. R. W. Smail Professor of History at the University of Wisconsin, Madison. I've made copies of that for you all to take home to your Meetings."

The following citations represent the information John presented and passed on, although any single topic may be covered in a multitude of other books, magazine articles, news stories, and internet presentations. And there is not a one-to-one correspondence to all information that would make possible a set of numbered end notes.

Please check out the QUIT website and blog, www.quit-torture-now.org, and the audio talks available through QUIT.

---

Cole, Juan (June 6, 2011). *Informed Comment: Thoughts on the Middle East, History, and Religion.* Ellsberg: All Nixon's Crimes Against Me Now Legal. Retrieved from: http://www.juancole.com/2011/06/ellsberg-all-nixons-crimes-against-me-now-legal.html. Pentagon Papers and current law criminalizing dissent.

Harbury, Jennifer K., *Truth, Torture, and the American Way: The History and Consequences of U.S. Involvement in Torture.* (Beacon Press, Boston, 2005). The Viet Nam position.

Hochschild, Arlie (June 29, 2005). Arrested Development. *New York Times Op Ed.* Retrieved from: http://www.nytimes.com/2005/06/29/opinion/29hochschild.html?_r=0. Children detained in American prisons in Afghanistan, Iraq and Guantánamo Bay.

Horton, Scott (June 7, 2010). Bush-era Human Experimentation Program Revealed. *Harper's Magazine.* Retrieved from: http://harpers.org/blog/2010/06/bush-era-cia-human-experimentation-program-revealed/.

Horton, Scott (September 3, 2010). When is Offering a Drink of Water a Crime? *Harper's Magazine*. Retrieve from: http://harpers.org/blog/2010/09/when-is-offering-a-drink-of-water-a-crime/.

Kaye, Jeffrey (April 19, 2011). *Truthout*. Guantánamo Psychologist Led Rendition and Imprisonment of Afghan Boys, Complaint Charges. Retrieved from: http://truth-out.org/author/itemlist/user/44741. Rendition and imprisonment of Afghan boys. Medical experiments. Camp Iguana.

McCoy, Alfred W., *A Question of Torture: CIA Interrogation, from the Cold War to the War on Terror*. (New York: Henry Holt and Company, LLC, 2006). Medical experimentation; water methods and "waterboarding"; School of the Americas; Nuremberg Code, Article Four; Central Intelligence Agency (CIA).

Reid, Tim (April 20, 2010). *London Times*. George W. Bush 'knew Guantánamo prisoners were innocent.' Retrieved from http://www.memeorandum.com/100409/p44#a100409p44.

Truthout Investigative Report (December 20, 2010). *Truthout*. EXCLUSIVE: Controversial Drug Given to All Guantánamo Detainees Akin to "Pharmacological Waterboarding" Retrieved from: http://www.truth-out.org/archive/item/93140:exclusive-controversial-drug-given-to-all-guantanamo-detainees-akin-to-pharmacologic-waterboarding .
Waterboarding. Medical experimentation over years at Guantánamo.

# Permissions and Credits

## Permissions

All written material in this book has been given by permission of the agencies named.

Permission has been given to John Calvi to use actual names of living persons in some pieces. Judicious naming of persons no longer living has been used. At times names have been removed or stylized in such a way as to protect the privacy of individuals.

## Speeches

Speeches and previously published articles have been modified to fit the requirements of this book. Some talks are available in audio format. To some extent the cadence and tone of John's spoken words have been reworked by him or with his permission to make reading flow more easily.

Section 1, "The Dance Between Hope & Fear," was initially a keynote speech delivered on July 4 at the 1990 Friends General Conference Gathering at Carlton College in Carlton, Minnesota. The speech was reprinted in 2003 by Friends for Lesbian, Gay, Bisexual, Transgender, and Queer Concerns (formerly known as Friends for Lesbian and Gay Concerns), *Each of Us Inevitable*, Revised, Expanded Edition, edited by Robert Leuze under the title "Laying Down the Weapons 'Round Our Hearts." An internet version is available at flgbtqc.quaker.org/eachofus.

Section 4, "Flowing Waters from the Source," was initially a plenary speech delivered to Friends World Committee for Consultation, Peace Conference, February 2003, Guilford College, Greensboro, N.C.

Section 8, "Healing America, Ending Torture: To Go Where There Is No Light," was the opening plenary speech at the 2011 Friends General Conference Gathering at Grinnell College in Grinnell, Iowa. The speech is available on CD through Quaker Books of FGC, www.quakerbooks.org.

## Publications

"Still Learning" was published in *Peace Team News*, Winter 2000, Vol. 5, Issue 1. Val Liveoak, editor.

"Did It Hurt to Listen" was published in *Out in the Mountains* GLBTQ Newspaper of Vermont, March 2000.

## Songs

*A Little Gracefulness.* Music and lyrics copyright by John Calvi, 1981. Recorded by The Short Sisters, 1997.

*The Ones Who Aren't Here.* Music and lyrics copyright by John Calvi, 1982. Recorded by Meg Christian at Carnegie Hall, 1982, *Meg/Cris at Carnegie Hall [Live]*; recorded by Suede, 1988, *Easily Suede.*

Transcriptions of John Calvi songs in this book were prepared by Richard Stout.

# Glossary of Quaker Terms

The definitions below are provided to clarify Quaker terminology and phrases used in this book for readers who are not Quakers; they are short, and they are sometimes specific to this book; a few have been borrowed from Quaker Information Service of Earlham School of Religion (http://www.quakerinfo.org). The terms are common within unprogrammed Friends, the branch of the Society of Friends John Calvi comes from, and do not represent all groups called by the names Friends or Quakers.

*Advices and Queries*: Guidance and questions to help Friends examine themselves and their lives as they strive to live more fully in the Light.

*Clearness Committee*: A Quaker clearness committee is initiated by an individual or individuals who wish to have a personal or familial situation, a leading, or a concern made more spiritually clear before taking action. The primary function of a clearness committee is to listen and assist with discernment. (See Threshing Session for group clearness process.)

*Clerk*: The clerk of a Meeting performs an administrative function in a way that provides spiritual leadership. Clerks act in a capacity similar to a chairperson during and between business Meetings. Usually a clerk is nominated by a committee, approved by the full body, and serves a specified term, after which another clerk is appointed.

*Concern*: A deeply-felt and Divinely inspired sense of personal responsibility to do something about a situation or problem or need. (See Leading.)

*Continuing Revelation*: Friends believe that the Divine Spirit, God, Light continues to make itself known directly if they listen expectantly and patiently for the "still small voice." In some Friends' traditions, such an unmediated opening is more highly valued and sought after than the teachings of tradition, clergy, or Scripture. (See Concern, Opening, and Leading.)

*Faith and Practice*: Also called Disciplines or Book of Discipline. Each Yearly Meeting creates or adopts its own book of discipline describing "good order used among us." Typically, contents include the practices and procedures used in the Yearly Meeting, inspirational extracts from Quaker literature, and Advices and Queries.

*Friends General Conference*: FGC is an association of regional Quaker organizations primarily in the United States and Canada. Founded in 1900, FGC has grown from a voluntary organization of seven Yearly Meetings, created to hold a "general conference" every other year, to an association of fourteen Yearly Meetings, supplemented with regional groups and individual Meetings. FGC continues to sponsor an annual Gathering of Friends. Sections 1 and 8 of this book are speeches given by John Calvi at FGC Gathering.

*Leading*: A sense of being called by Spirit to undertake a specific course of action. Very often in early times leadings led to travel. Leadings often arise from a concern.

*Light*: We invite you to search the internet to find the many phrases and understandings commonly used within the Religious Society of Friends. For understanding the use of "Light" in this book, the simplest definition might be that of Rufus Jones, Quaker historian and theologian of the early 20th century, who wrote: "The Inner Light is the doctrine that there is something Divine, 'Something of God' in the human soul." (See Continuing Revelation.)

*Meeting*: Among many Friends, the word "church" is not used, and the word "Meeting" often serves the same function. A Meeting may be the body of people who constitute a congregation, or it may be an event in which Friends come together to worship or carry out other group activities in anticipation of a spiritual encounter with Divine Spirit and one another.

- Meeting for Worship: In the largest sense, all meetings are Meetings for Worship. Used by itself, the term signifies a Quaker Meeting where people gather to wait upon the Light, and if they are led, may rise and speak. Meeting for Worship can be thought of as a Quaker church service, but there is no ritual, no order of service, no plan, and no religious leader. Meeting for Business is short for "Meeting for worship with a concern for business" or "Meeting for worship for business."

In Business Meeting, decisions are made together through worshipful attention to the Spirit and deep listening to one another; no voting occurs. Worship Groups are usually small gatherings of Friends in isolated areas or coming together without the structure of Business Meetings. Other types of meetings may be held, such as memorial meetings, celebratory meetings (as when the birth of a child is celebrated or when a couple is married under the care of the Meeting), and "eating meeting" (almost always potluck).

- Monthly Meeting is the term used to describe a Friends' congregation (e.g., Dallas Monthly Meeting). British Friends call their congregations "Preparative Meetings" and several of them come together monthly to have meeting for business.

- Quarterly Meeting is the term applied to an association of Monthly Meetings within a more-or-less local region. [American terminology]

- Yearly Meeting refers to a larger body of Friends, consisting of Monthly Meetings and Worship Groups in a general geographic area connected with the same branch of Friends. For most purposes, a Yearly Meeting is as high as Quaker organizational structure goes. Members of Yearly Meetings come together regulary (not necessarily on an annual basis) for fellowship and spiritual enrichment. Friends, like John Calvi, are often invited to give plenary talks, workshops, or other activities at Yearly Meetings. As an example of the variety and scope of Yearly Meetings, Canadian Yearly Meeting encompasses all of Canada; South Central Yearly Meeting (USA) encompasses Texas, Oklahoma, Arkansas, and Louisiana and is composed mostly of a number of very small meetings and worship groups; while Philadelphia Yearly Meeting is made up of over one hundred local meeting communities in Eastern Pennsylvania, Southern New Jersey, all of Delaware and Eastern Maryland. Intervisitation and events between the various levels of meetings and Yearly Meetings is critical in keeping alive smaller and more geographically distant groups.

- Meeting House: The meeting house is the building in which a Monthly Meeting gathers for worship and other community activities; a meeting house is not necessary for Friends' worship or gatherings.

*Opening*: A Divinely inspired recognition of some truth. (See Continuing Revelation.)

*Programmed/Unprogrammed Worship*: The Quaker Meetings and Gatherings described in this book take place, for the most part, in communities of unprogrammed Friends. John Calvi's work has taken him to many venues outside of Quaker gatherings as well as within both programmed and unprogrammed Friends' gatherings.

- Programmed Worship is practiced by Friends in much of the U.S. and Africa, as well as in South and Central America and other locations. It is similar in many ways to Protestant church services and is led by a pastor, or someone acting in the role of a pastor.

- Unprogrammed Worship, the practice of early Friends, is continued in much of the English-speaking world, Europe, and former British colonies, as well as various other locations. The participants gather in silence and worshippers seek to be receptive to the Divine Spirit through the Inward Light. If vocal ministry is offered, it is done so spontaneously by any worshipper who feels called by the Spirit to speak.

*Threshing Session*: At times a significant number of Friends might find themselves in disagreement, even after following the corporate methods of listening inwardly for Light, and it appears that no resolution through ordinary Quakerly means can take place. A threshing session may be established to honor the differences within the body and to strengthen understanding. Decisions are not made at a threshing session. An excellent article on how Friends might proceed in a period of disagreement can be found at http://www.friendsjournal.org/2010090/.
(Compare to Clearness Committee.)


*Wear it as long as thou canst*: A story has come down from early times, factual or not, that when William Penn first embraced Quakerism, he asked George Fox if he might still wear his sword, which was a sign of social rank. Fox is said to have answered, "Wear it as long as thou canst." Whether or not the story is factual, it carries great truth for Friends. When John Calvi tells a friend with AIDS, who says he hasn't given up yet, to "wear it as long as thou canst" he is bringing all that he and his friend know of goodness, uncertainty, and Spirit to the forefront of their relationship.

# How Do You Say Thank You to Thousands?

There are many many people who have helped me to come to now, today, my life's work, and this book. The people who have given me learning, shelter, food, transport, and encouragement are more numerous than can be named. Learning a gift of healing has been a long path that continues for me. And my decades thus far have depended on the kindness of kindred seekers who want to see healing in a world broken and beautiful. While I cannot name everyone here, I can tell you that I have welcome in every corner of the country where I know where the spare key is, what time the llamas are fed, how the hosts take their Gin and Tonic, where the snakes live near the basement dryer, whose war taxes await government retrieval, which window is to be left unlocked for the secret lover, where the asthma medicine is kept, whose truck was a stud magnet, what months the chocolate truffles are made, whose wife knows about the boyfriend, who mistook Alaska for Arkansas, which cousin has the best sex stories, whose cat cannot go out and whose dog cannot come in, who can spare emergency cash, who has time but no money, who can offer quiet and understands solitude as deep need, who throws the best parties, who doesn't need me at my public best, and who understands restoration and will hide me until I am rested and reasonable once again.

In my time of living on gifts and working by invitation I have been given food, housing, cars, scholarship, cash, credit, loans, clothing, gas, and blankets. Thirty years of living through the kindness and generosity of others is in itself a spiritual discipline of expectation and gratitude—my best will be seen and requested in a way that will provide what is needed to go on and do more. It's not been poverty so much as suspense, and this has always been answered by kindness, genuine help, and the reassurance of sharing wealth of various kinds.

I have also received the invaluable gift of trust. Each time I'm invited into someone's life for healing work, their trust of me in our seeking together is a gift beyond measure. Not only is their trust a balm to my life, it is the permission to study what we see and understand. This has been a world library above any collection imaginable. I am grateful to receive this gift and acknowledge its importance here.

There is one person to be acknowledged by name in the making of this book. I have never known such a person until now. Who could even dream up a person that would come out of the blue to say—give me everything you've written in the past thirty years, I'm going to make your first book! And that this person would be very computer literate and an excellent editor of the written word and devote a couple of years to a project larger than I could imagine or dare take on myself. Plus she could speak to a very learning-disabled author whose gifts lie far, very far, from spelling, grammar, punctuation, sentence and paragraph construction, and show me that my part was to clarify meaning and she would take care of the rest. And there were oodles of "the rest." She not only transcribed hours of recordings and scanned handwritten notes scribbled over decades, she also made sure my machines at home were tops and appropriate to the task, including providing several of them. We met for weeks here and there, mostly there, with her careful agenda prepared ahead and paced to my distractible wee brain while she ran ahead preparing the ground for the next stages. Can't imagine anyone else putting up with all this and in the tone of all the kindness and generosity and patience of a delighted angel. Anyone else would have left screaming in frustration before Section 2.

Shelly Angel provided an extraordinary gift to tell an extreme story. There would be no book without her good and gracious talents, intentions, and true Quaker ways. For this I am very grateful. We are a couple of laughing co-conspirators, very happy to be on the road together.

Made in the USA
San Bernardino, CA
18 April 2015